The BHS
Instructors' Manual for
TEACHING
RIDING

The BHS Instructors' Manual for

TEACHING RIDING

THE BRITISH HORSE SOCIETY

ISLAY AUTY FBHS

KENILWORTH PRESS

First published in the UK in 2003
by Kenilworth Press, an imprint of Quiller Publishing Ltd

Reprinted 2005, 2007

British Library Cataloguing-in-Publication Data
A catalogue record for this book
is available from the British Library

ISBN 978 1 872119 56 4

Layout by Kenilworth Press
Line drawings in main text (except p 6) by Dianne Breeze
Diagrams in lesson plans by Michael J Stevens

Printed in Great Britain by Bell & Bain, Glasgow

Kenilworth Press

An imprint of Quiller Publishing Ltd
Wykey House, Wykey, Shrewsbury, SY4 1JA
Tel: 01939 261616 Fax: 01939 261606
E-mail: info@quillerbooks.com
Website: www.kenilworthpress.co.uk

Contents

BHS Qualifications

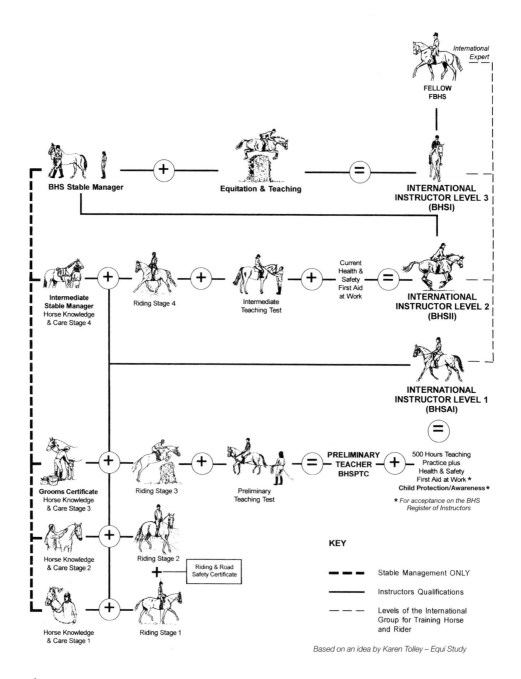

International
Expert

**FELLOW
FBHS**

BHS Stable Manager ⊕ **Equitation & Teaching** ⊜ **INTERNATIONAL
INSTRUCTOR LEVEL 3
(BHSI)**

**Intermediate
Stable Manager**
Horse Knowledge
& Care Stage 4 ⊕ Riding Stage 4 ⊕ **Intermediate
Teaching Test** ⊕ Current
Health &
Safety
First Aid
at Work ⊜ **INTERNATIONAL
INSTRUCTOR LEVEL 2
(BHSII)**

**INTERNATIONAL
INSTRUCTOR LEVEL 1
(BHSAI)**

⊜

Grooms Certificate
Horse Knowledge
& Care Stage 3 ⊕ Riding Stage 3 ⊕ Preliminary
Teaching Test ⊜ **PRELIMINARY
TEACHER
BHSPTC** ⊕ 500 Hours Teaching
Practice plus
Health & Safety
First Aid at Work ✱
Child Protection/Awareness ✱

✱ *For acceptance on the BHS
Register of Instructors*

Horse Knowledge
& Care Stage 2 ⊕ Riding Stage 2

Riding & Road
Safety Certificate

Horse Knowledge
& Care Stage 1 ⊕ Riding Stage 1

KEY

▬ ▬ ▬ Stable Management ONLY

────── Instructors Qualifications

─ ─ ─ Levels of the International
Group for Training Horse
and Rider

Based on an idea by Karen Tolley – Equi Study

Introduction – A Few Definitions

EQUESTRIAN SPORT IS MOVING TOWARDS defining more clearly the names it uses to identify its educators. At present riders can learn with trainers (particularly in dressage), coaches, instructors and teachers. *Chambers Twentieth-Century Dictionary* identifies these terms as follows:

Trainer: (in the case of riding) someone who produces horses (and riders) ultimately for competition; **training**: practical education in riding.

Instructor: teacher, one who informs, prepares or conveys knowledge.

Teacher: one who informs or imparts knowledge; one whose profession is or talent is to convey knowledge.

Coach: a private tutor, instructor; one who tutors or instructs.

The British Horse Society qualifications – for 'instructors' – have been around for about fifty years and are well known both nationally and internationally. The term 'instructor' probably has its origins in the military where all teachers were known as instructors. As a professional label, it is probably here to stay for the foreseeable future.

When a person takes up a new activity (in this case riding, but it applies equally to driving cars, learning to play tennis, etc.) he or she needs to acquire basic skills in that chosen subject. Those skills are taught by a teacher or instructor. In riding, pupils learns the basic tools of how to mount, dismount, sit, stop, start, turn, etc. As they progress and gain experience, the number of new skills they need to learn reduces and they move into the area of consolidation and development of expertise. When the rider takes on the commitment to become a competitive rider (at any level) he or she may benefit from the skills of a coach or trainer, who works with the existing skills and develops the quality and expertise to as high a level as talent, opportunity, horse power, time, etc. will allow.

I have deliberately used the two terms **instructor** and **teaching** in the title of this book. Our professionals are firstly **instructors** or **teachers**; they are **teaching riding**; they are educating the beginner or less experienced rider; they may, in due course, take their riders further to a competitive stage and then regard themselves as a **coach** or a **trainer**, or pass those riders on to a more specialist coach or trainer.

1 Qualities of a Riding Instructor

BEFORE WE CONSIDER THE QUALITIES THAT ARE USEFUL to a good riding instructor we should first consider **why** you teach or might want to teach:

- To earn a living. (There are easier, more lucrative ways of earning money!)

- You have a genuine desire to pass on to others the sense of satisfaction that you enjoy as a rider.

- You enjoy generating enthusiasm in other riders.

- You take pleasure from witnessing the sense of satisfaction and achievement that your pupils get from riding.

As a riding instructor, what qualities are going to be useful to you?

- Knowledge of and a passion for your subject.

- A genuine liking for people and a desire to inspire them.

- A caring personality.

- A desire to impart your knowledge and ability to others.

- Ability as a rider, because this helps you understand the possible problems that a rider might have.

- Enthusiasm and stamina.

- A clear voice and one that is easy to listen to.

- A sense of humour.

- Sensitivity to the variations in moods of your riders and their horses.

- The ability to convey information with clarity and encouragement.

- The acuity to spot minor and major faults, and the ability to be able quickly to offer a practical correction so that the rider can act on it swiftly.

- Self-confidence, as this will instil greater confidence in your pupil(s).

- The ability to convey information in a form that is simple enough for an inexperienced person to appreciate the value of the lesson.

- The ability to give praise where praise is due, and to offer criticism in a constructive way; in this way the rider's self-esteem is maintained and the desire to work harder to improve is instilled.

Teaching style

How should you teach?

- With **authority** and effective control in every situation.

- With **awareness**. This commodity is **absolutely** essential in any form of work with horses. Awareness comes from spending a lot of time around horses in every situation. Horses are not 'big' thinking animals; they are browsers and grazers and learn by repetition. Inevitably they retain the knowledge of bad experiences as readily as good feelings. It is therefore a great advantage to be able to develop a feeling for, or an awareness of, how a horse reacts in different circumstances. This is something that comes with practice and a constant commitment to being able to 'read' horses better. For example, a horse with his ears flat back on his neck and looking mean and fierce, is upset by something or someone 'in his space'. A reassuring pat on the neck and an awareness of the 'thing' in the vicinity that might have disturbed him, will help you to defuse the tension in the horse – a condition that is usually counterproductive to the rider.

- With **empathy** and **sympathy**. As a teacher you have to 'care' about your pupils. You need to develop an empathy for their feelings in any situation. Clients tend to bring their worries and emotions with them to their lessons, and this can have a direct effect on your ability to impart knowledge to them. However, once you understand this it can help you to create an environment that is more conducive to learning. For example, if a child arrives at a class lesson having just had a row with, say, her mother, she may still be tense and anxious when she starts to ride. And if you then try to encourage relaxation during the lesson you may find yourself battling against a hidden problem.

- With **enthusiasm**. There are days when enthusiasm is easier to muster than others. Try to remember that for weekly riders their one-hour lesson is extremely precious to them. It is the highlight of their week and something they look forward to with increasing anticipation. When they arrive for the lesson and find that you are grumpy and irritable for whatever reason (perhaps you fell out with boy/girlfriend, or your horse went badly when you schooled it, or you've been standing in the cold and wet teaching for four hours already!) they are justifiably disappointed and their expectations of the lesson are dashed. In the long term this is not in anyone's interests. Your pupils will quickly become disillusioned, blame you for their lack of enjoyment or progress and may even give up riding – which will ultimately affect your livelihood. Enthusiasm is therefore an essential commodity in any teacher. You must learn to be able to produce it at some stage in every lesson, even if it is the furthest thought from your mind. It is part of the professionalism that is required in a valued riding instructor.

- With **confidence**. Confidence evolves with the success you achieve with your pupils, at any level. Once you find that you can develop a rider's skills, that classes enjoy your teaching, and that there is a good two-way communication between yourself and your pupils, you become increasingly confident in your ability. As confidence grows you become braver in using your skills as a teacher. Moreover, your confidence quickly inspires confidence in your pupils, and the whole lesson environment becomes a platform for learning and growth.

- With **knowledge**. Committed teachers are always seeking to learn more themselves so that they can impart greater knowledge to their pupils. Improving your own knowledge is usually a very stimulating experience, and this in turn can be used to motivate your own pupils. When you become reluctant to seek continuous personal development (CPD) your own teaching is likely to reach a plateau status where motivation and interest may become stationary. (See ways of pursuing CPD, page 18.)

- With **stamina** and **patience**. These two attributes can be considered together as well as independently. As a riding instructor you will be working in an outdoor environment for a large part of your working life. When you teach outside you will have to deal with the elements – wind, rain, sun and, perhaps at times, snow! Even if you work in an indoor school, these can be notoriously cold in winter and often hot in summer. You will therefore need to have stamina and staying power. In bad weather it is essential that you can stay warm and, if possible, dry, because teaching when you are cold and/or wet is miserable in the extreme.

Patience is certainly a much-needed attribute. There will be times when a rider appears to take forever to grasp (what seems to you) a simple task or exercise – and you will need patience to work through the problem. Always lay the blame at your own door if a rider is confused about something you are teaching him. Consider whether:

(a) you have explained the task clearly;

(b) the rider is capable of carrying out the instructions you have given;

(c) the horse is able to carry out the task if the rider asks sufficiently clearly.

Try to avoid demonstrating irritation with your pupil. Be patient. If necessary, try approaching the task from a different angle or use another member of the ride to demonstrate what you are aiming for.

Lesson content

As a general principle you should 'teach what you see in front of you'. In other words, on the day, as you initially assess your rider's (or riders') competence you make a mental plan of what you will teach based on the abilities and weaknesses that you see during the assessment. In reality there will be variations on that principle. The following reasons may influence the general plan of the lesson:

- The rider has specifically booked, for example, a jumping lesson, a lunge lesson, a cross-country lesson, or a hack.

- The rider is in a group lesson that will be more generally directed to the overall skill of the group rather than the individual needs of one specific rider.

- The rider has aspirations to progress because he or she has a near goal approaching (e.g. a competition or an impending exam).

Whatever the situation, however, you must **NEVER** be pressurised, either by a rider or his close associates (parents, friend, etc.), into tackling work which you feel is well beyond the ability of the rider and which may therefore put him in a potentially unsafe situation. You, as the instructor in charge of a lesson, must always be able to justify why you chose a specific area of work or exercise for the rider(s) you were teaching. **NEVER** be tempted to do something with a rider(s) that you feel uncomfortable about.

The **timing** of what you teach is critical to confidence and the safe development of riders. Linked to the points made above as a result of the assessment of the rider(s) on the day, decisions can be made about what work can be attempted and, it is hoped, achieved in the ensuing lesson. Depending on the ability and knowledge of the rider(s) the work should be generally agreed between the teacher and the pupil(s). Obviously this is not reasonable with beginner or novice riders who will not have the experience to choose what work might be appropriate.

Teaching facilities

Where you teach will depend on the facilities available to you. These may range from a large well-appointed indoor school to the corner of a windy field. Where you are teaching may influence 'what' you teach. It is easy to teach a first canter lesson in a quiet, secure indoor school with a good, consistent surface. It is very different trying to teach that same lesson in an outdoor school on a cold, windy day with horses running around in the field next door. The facilities and conditions that you work in must play a part in your lesson planning in the interests of safety and confidence for your pupils.

2 Becoming an Instructor

THERE ARE SEVERAL WELL-DEFINED PATHWAYS towards becoming a riding instructor. Whichever route you take, there is no substitute for practical 'hands-on' experience. Ultimately the more experience you gain, as long as you maintain an open and enquiring attitude to the inevitable changes that evolve in any profession, the more proficient you should be as an instructor.

Training in a 'Where to Train' centre

Following a practical apprenticeship-type of training in a commercial riding school/training centre offers the trainee the opportunity to learn in a genuine working-business environment. The British Horse Society, the recognised body for teaching qualifications in the equine industry in Great Britain, runs an approval scheme whereby commercial riding schools are inspected for the standard of training they offer to career students. Establishments approved under this scheme are known as 'Where to Train' centres, and the scheme runs adjacent to that for the approval of riding schools, where inspected schools are approved as 'Where to Ride' schools.

Each training centre operates its own individual training programme, which is broadly based on a one- or two-year period where the trainee works 'on the job' whilst receiving daily training towards The British Horse Society professional examinations (see page 6). At the end of the training period, the student should be aiming to achieve The British Horse Society Preliminary Teaching Test. When the candidate passes the PTT and the Stage 3 exam, and accumulates 500 hours of practical teaching experience, he or she is awarded the BHSAI (Assistant Instructor) certificate. The student will almost certainly have been steadily gaining some initial teaching practice, under supervision, in the school.

Training in a college

Many colleges around the UK run equine-related courses for students of all ages and backgrounds. Students may attend full-time from the age of sixteen (having just left school) to any upper age, and some students may attend on a day-release or evening-course basis. Equine college courses include other subjects such as IT (information technology), numeracy skills, business management and related competencies. Student numbers tend to be much larger than those in commercial riding centres, leading some students to feel that they lack an 'individual approach'.

Courses can cover any standard, from first diploma to degree level. (See list of college qualifications, page 142.) On the whole, the higher the academic standard required by the course, the less 'hands-on' practical work there is likely to be time for, and students may find that they do not ride every day.

Many equine colleges offer high-quality facilities and employ well-qualified (and usually industrially experienced) staff. The bigger colleges run regular competitions, giving students the chance to experience the commercial aspect of a competition centre.

Colleges offer a more formal structured regime of training than many commercial centres, which, for their part, provide a genuine insight into the ups and downs of running a riding school through the seasons. Most colleges direct their students towards British Horse Society qualifications, albeit alongside a college certification or a National Vocational Qualification (NVQ) or Scottish National Vocational Qualification (SNVQ).

Industrial experience

A small number of instructors enter the industry through experience alone. Three or four decades ago, many instructors came into private or commercial teaching through an earlier military background. Such a route is rare today.

Some people develop skill and competence as a rider and then gradually slip into teaching, almost by accident. Success as a competitor often causes others who admire or wish to emulate that success to approach that individual for lessons or training. Many riders then find that teaching can be highly rewarding, and not without benefits financially.

Not all good riders automatically make good teachers, due to their inability to break down tasks into a form of instruction that less-competent riders can understand and put into practice. Some riders, however, find teaching to be both challenging and rewarding, and therefore certainly worth doing and developing. Apart from the financial incentive, there is a large amount of satisfaction in seeing pupil(s) develop under your guidance.

There are disadvantages to not holding formal qualifications, though. In this increasingly litigious world, insurance as an instructor is imperative. Qualifications that endorse or reflect your experience are increasingly required as a 'bench mark' of competence. Insurance will safeguard you in any situation, should the worst happen and you are involved in a court action. In addition to equine-specific two-day first-aid courses offered by The British Horse Society, 'child protection' courses are also run to enable instructors to appreciate the issues they need to be aware of in the care, supervision and training of children (see Duty of Care booklet – page 142). Instructors with a BHS qualification can join the BHS Register of Instructors, which offers a competitive rate of insurance for all members. It also promotes continuous personal development on a regular basis by running training courses, conventions and lectures all at a reduced rate for those on the Register and holding a BHS qualification. Teachers who have only their own experience to rely on need to be constantly in the 'public eye' to ensure that clients 'remember' them and keep using them.

The British Horse Society Instructor qualification pathway is shown on page 6. It is a matter for debate as to whether qualifications or experience produce the most competent teacher. In the author's opinion the vital ingredients are a mix of formal training as a 'teacher' combined with practical experience in the industry and an over-riding passion to want to help others achieve the fun and satisfaction that the sport gives us. Today, though, there is increased pressure, particularly as a result of increased litigation, to encourage all instructors in sport to hold a recognised (national governing body) qualification.

Responsibilities of the instructor and the pupil

THE INSTRUCTOR'S RESPONSIBILITIES
As a teacher you have huge responsibilities to your pupil(s). Your responsibilities are to:

- Impart correct knowledge. Technically incorrect information will ultimately confuse your pupils when they encounter the 'truth'.

- Carefully assess your riders' competence at each stage. You have the responsibility not to be over-demanding in this respect; to do so might cause a set-back and subsequent loss of confidence.

- Maintain the trust and confidence of your pupils.

- Be fair and truthful to them. When they ask questions, be honest in a constructive way.

- **NEVER** underestimate your pupils. **NEVER** make a final judgement of what their capabilities are. Sometimes their determination and drive may take them to levels you could never have expected.

- Never be sarcastic or make pupils feel inadequate or 'silly' in front of you or a group of other riders.

- Never demoralise your pupils.

- Gauge the fitness and confidence of your pupils and work them accordingly.

THE PUPIL'S RESPONSIBILITIES

In teaching, often there is a perception that success is achieved in direct relation to the input and expertise of the teacher. But, no matter how good the teacher, no one ever learned to play the piano well through being taught for an hour a week, with no practising of the scales and dexterity on the keys between lessons. And most riding pupils are weekly riders without the opportunity to practise during the week. This means that progress is very gradual. The weekly rider can, however, help himself by reading up about the level of work at which he is currently working. He can also help his co-ordination and suppleness by doing exercises at home (or in the gym). Swimming and cycling will also improve the fitness and suppleness, thus helping the pupil ride better during his one hour's lesson per week.

During a lesson the rider's responsibility to the teacher is as great as the teacher's commitment to the pupil. If the rider makes little or no effort to carry out the work suggested, then progress is likely to be limited or non-existent. The pupil must believe in the instructor, have confidence in him and make an effort to fulfil his suggestions. If there is a conflict of personalities then this should be discussed and attempts made to resolve it. Progress can only be possible if there is an equal and opposite commitment – from the pupil to the teacher and from the teacher to the pupil – mutually working together towards an agreed goal of achievement.

Continuous personal development (CPD)

Teaching is about giving: giving something of yourself every time you teach. You need some replenishment on a regular basis to keep your motivation and enthusiasm positive. Whatever you choose for your own CPD will be partly appropriate to your own standard as an instructor currently and partly related to whatever else you are doing in your equestrian life. For example, you may be competing, in which case a lesson with your own horse from time to time stimulates your drive to improve. Attending a convention or clinic may give you further motivation to take your teaching skills forward. Whatever you choose, it should give you some incentive to improve, and to pass on that improvement in your teaching.

Taking care of yourself

As a working instructor you should demonstrate a consideration for yourself and your own well-being. Notoriously we often work long and anti-social hours. It is therefore important to try to eat regularly and to opt for well-balanced meals. Chocolate, crisps and cola are not conducive to providing the body with a good balance of nutrients. A sudden energy rush (from ingested sugar, such as chocolate) will inevitably be followed by a 'down' feeling. This is because your blood-sugar runs low. Instead you need to give your body slow-energy-releasing food to provide you with a steady input of calories to last you through your next two or three hours of teaching.

Try to train yourself to snack on fruit instead of sugary foods, and drink plenty of water (not fizzy drinks!), particularly when it is hot or humid and you are losing a large amount of fluid through sweating (whether you realise you are or not). Eat some breakfast every day, and have one 'proper' meal at some time during the day. In between, keep 'topped up' on fruit and drink water freely. Avoid too much tea and coffee. And keep off cigarettes – they don't do your breathing or your voice any good in the long run!

Insurance

If you are an instructor with a BHS qualification and a member of the BHS Register of Instructors, then as a Category 'A' instructor you will have insurance for public liability, which will cover you in the event of an accident where an injured party felt he or she could claim negligence against you. If you are registered under the Category B scheme, then your insurance cover is effected by the riding school for which you work and you are **NOT** covered by your Register membership. Should you choose to carry out instruction for Pony Clubs or BHS-affiliated Riding Clubs, then you are covered by their insurance; but if you teach private individuals then you should ensure that you take out adequate personal insurance with a reputable company to give you peace of mind in your professional work.

3 Communication

T
O BE ABLE TO IMPART KNOWLEDGE to another person you must be able to communicate that information in some way. The main form of communication used as an instructor is the voice.

Voice

If you are going to earn your living as a riding instructor for many years, you must learn to use your voice effectively and with due regard for the vital tool that it is in your line of work. It helps considerably if you naturally have a strong voice, but this is not essential – and often if you do have a deep or strong voice as a God-given commodity you are accused of shouting! Shouting should **NEVER** be part of the instructor's repertoire. You must learn to project your voice but not shout.

Learning to use your voice correctly involves good breathing. You must learn to breathe deeply from the base of your diaphragm, expanding your lungs to maximum capacity and controlling the way in which the air is expelled. Control of the expelled air will help you to be able to regulate the resonance, consistency and strength of your voice.

If you need help in this area, it may help you to talk to a drama or singing teacher, since they are trained to encourage their pupils to make maximum use of their voices efficiently and without strain.

The following simple guidelines should help you to utilise your voice more efficiently and correctly:

- Learn to breathe in deeply and slowly, expanding your lungs as fully as you can.

- Expel air gradually and slowly as a controlled exercise so that your pattern of breathing becomes deeper and more effective; this will follow through into the use of your voice.

- Learn to 'throw' your voice, not from the back of your throat in a 'shout' but from much deeper in your chest.

- Regulate your words so that they do not rush out quickly at the beginning, when you have lots of air in a new breath, and then fade and slow down at the end as you lose air.

- Learn to breathe within sentences, where necessary, and use a 'pause' to good effect within a sentence.

- Silence can be a useful and powerful teaching aid; it allows your riders thinking time for themselves.

- Remember that surfaces (indoor and outdoor) often absorb the voice. Learn to project your voice upwards and forwards; avoid looking down and allowing your voice to go 'down' into the school surface.

- Learn to keep each sentence as strong at the end as it is at the beginning. Some inexperienced teachers speak loudly at the start of a command and then fade to nothing towards the end of the words.

- Think of where your riders are when you are directing words to them. If they are moving directly away from you, they are unlikely to hear you. Wind and rain will also greatly affect the volume of your voice. Gusty wind is the worst because it grabs your voice and carries it away from you.

- Learn to speak slowly and clearly, making each of your words crisp and well enunciated.

- Make use of given opportunities to talk to your ride, such as when you line them up and before you send them off again to work.

Your voice is one of your greatest assets as a teacher. Look after it and avoid teaching in excessively dusty environments. If you have a heavy day's teaching, try to follow it with an easy day afterwards to rest your voice. It has to last you a lifetime. If you teach a lot of private lessons, consider investing in a small two-way radio system, whereby you can speak privately and quietly through a radio microphone to your rider, who has a small radio receiver and earpiece through which to hear you. This is ideal at a competition venue when working in a rider.

Body language

Body language is another great asset in teaching, and its use is as relevant to the teacher as it is to the pupil.

Let us consider some of aspects of body language and what they tell us:

- Body language is the message or messages that your body stance, position and movement send out to horse and/or rider. Similarly their body language is sending signals back to you.

- An instructor who stands with his hands in his pockets, shoulders hunched, while constantly chatting to spectators and taking little interest in the ride, is showing an uninvolved and detached body language.

Both stances shown above indicate a negative attitude; and right, a total lack of interest in the pupil.

- An instructor who is enthusiastically moving towards a lazy pony in a joint effort with the rider to encourage him into canter in a corner, is showing an involved and committed body language.

- The body can exhibit tension, anxiety, excitement, anticipation, enthusiasm, anger, irritation and frustration, to name but a few emotions. Many of these will be seen in riders at different times while teaching.

- The instructor's body language can be a useful asset in assisting a horse/pony to be more co-operative about moving forward or slowing down if he is running away.

- The rider's body language is of great importance. It is the instructor's ongoing consideration to train the rider to control his body, both physically and emotionally, while on the horse at all times.

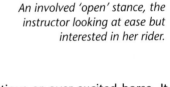

An involved 'open' stance, the instructor looking at ease but interested in her rider.

- The instructor's body language can demonstrate encouragement and enthusiasm. It can assist in creating energy to go forward, or can calm a fractious or over-excited horse. It can convey control and authority as required. It should never demonstrate lack of interest, irritation, anger or impatience, with either the horse or the rider.

Commands

Commands, or the way you convey information to your riders, are critical to the harmony and progression of the work. The commands you use with a trained school horse and a novice rider should facilitate the rider to adopt a clear system for control and information. (See also advice on using the voice, and body language, above.) Thus they need to be fairly consistent and formal. Your commands should be:

- Clearly delivered, so that the rider is quite sure of the response expected.

- Made with plenty of preparation and clear aid application.

- Most commands should be preceded by, 'Prepare to ...' followed by the necessary instruction.

Commands fall into two categories:

1. Informative, e.g. 'In succession, leading file trot to the rear of the ride.'

2. Executive, e.g. 'The whole ride, halt.'

Some commonly used commands might be:

- 'The whole ride, prepare to trot.'

- 'The ride, trot.'

- 'With X as leading file, the whole ride prepare to walk to the track in the following order: A, B, C, and D. At the track turn left. The whole ride walk march.'

- 'Leading file, in succession, trot and canter to the rear of the ride. Leading file commence.'

All commands must be clear and concise.

Further examples of how commands may be constructed can be found in the lesson plans at the back of the book.

Don't forget that **word of praise** and encouragement for the horse's response, especially after a light aid, will help maintain the morale and enthusiasm of the horse.

4 Understanding Horses and Riders

BECOMING A COMPETENT RIDING INSTRUCTOR/COACH/TEACHER is not just about teaching one athlete or performer, as in most other sports. It is about dealing with two independent beings (rider and horse), both of whom are breathing, thinking, feeling creatures. This places very different demands on you as a teacher. At your peril, you ignore the rider at the expense of the horse, and vice versa.

Understanding the horse

The ability to understand horses and their nature will greatly assist you when you are teaching riders, irrespective of the level. You must learn to 'read' the horse. The older the horse is (within reason) the more secure he is likely to be in what he knows; whereas the younger horse may be less reliable and unpredictable.

Let us consider how we can read or understand the horse. To do this we must be clear about what sort of animal he is and in what environment he feels most comfortable:

- The horse is a herd animal who likes to live non-aggressively in a group.

- He is by nature a herbivore and a browsing, grazing animal.

- He does not have a large brain in relation to his size, and has limited intelligence and reasoning power.

- He is fairly easily frightened.

- He learns through repetition and by imprinting information on his mind through habit.

- Given the choice, he will run away from what frightens him rather than confront it.

The horse demonstrates anxiety, nervousness or fear in any of the following ways:

- Ears back and an angry look on the face. Sometimes the horse 'wags' his head around, looking evil and opening his mouth slightly. Particularly he does this when he feels antagonistic towards another horse (or horses) which may be nearby.

- Tension through his body. To the rider, this will cause the horse's back to feel very stiff, and the horse may not be listening to his rider at all.

- Short, tense, choppy steps.

- Reluctance to go forward in any of his paces.

- 'Spooking' at 'hazards' (e.g. bin bags left out on the roadside or kerb side, or jumps left out in the school).

- Showing a desire to run away from anything 'scary'.

- He may resist or kick out against the rider's leg aids.

- He may swing his hindquarters in a resistant way.

- He may be fractious, not standing still or quietly, and occasionally may lift a hind leg.

Recognising the behaviour traits of the horses you use to teach riders and understanding what those traits might mean, will help you to establish harmony between horse and rider, particularly when teaching beginner or novice riders, who will have little or no understanding of what the horse they are riding is feeling or thinking.

Good 'school' horses are those that have learned to accept the variations that are inevitable from having different riders on their back, day in day out. They are generally quite long-suffering and show a tolerant attitude towards less-proficient riders. They tend to do only what is asked of them by the rider, but with a more competent rider they often 'raise their game,' and may perform or even compete at a surprisingly good level. A small percentage of horses never quite accept the variation of lots of different riders on board and show increasing reluctance to work. These horses should be re-homed as quickly as possible in a private home where the horse can enjoy being one person's 'special' horse.

It is your responsibility gradually to encourage your pupil(s) to develop their own awareness and understanding of how the horse is feeling and therefore how he might behave when ridden. For example, you can teach your beginner riders what the horse is telling them when:

- He nuzzles them with his nose with his ears forward.

- He puts his ears back and shakes his head when the girth is tightened or when the rider puts his toe into the horse's flank as he mounts.

In time, this knowledge will greatly improve the rider's sense of 'feel' for the horse and therefore their sense of timing and effect for better applying aids to the horse.

Understanding the rider

This may be a much more complex task than being able to read the horse; however, some degree of competence in this field is essential if you are to be a caring, perceptive, aware teacher.

Many riders (particularly weekly riders or those who ride purely for leisure) come to their weekly lesson with great expectations of that very precious riding time. They may also come with some other issues which may inhibit their ability to consciously apply themselves totally to the riding lesson. For example,

- A child may have fallen out with his/her mother on the journey to the lesson.

- A child may have had a demanding day at school and be mentally and physically tired when he/she comes to ride.

- An adult may have other worries on his mind when he/she comes to ride.

Riders display varying emotions either prior to riding or during the lesson which can demonstrate their mental state. For example, they may:

- Show anxiety about riding a certain horse (perhaps a new horse which they have not ridden before).

- Talk a great deal, or, conversely, be very quiet – both of these can indicate a nervousness which the rider may not admit to.

- Constantly tell you or others what they cannot do, focusing on their incompetence.

- Request not to jump, or to canter or to ride outside, or not to carry out any other specific equestrian activity which worries them.

Without singling out one rider, it is also important to encourage everyone in a class lesson to achieve to a similar standard. A small amount of competitive spirit can be useful to encourage the less-assertive, less-confident riders to strive for their best performance. Conversely, it is your responsibility to make sure that no member of a group is disadvantaged and left feeling that they are 'not as good' as one or more other members of the group.

In recognising and understanding the rider it is important that you consider the following:

- **The physique of the rider.** If a person isn't exactly built for riding, you have to work positively with what you've got. It is impossible to change the rider with, say, short arms or long legs. You must facilitate their improvement by helping them to sit as well as possible. They can then accommodate their own physical strengths or shortcomings by finding the best possible balance and co-ordination on the horse.

- **Rider fitness**. This is a major consideration because progress will be somewhat dictated by how fit the rider is and how often he rides. Beginner or novice riders who ride only once a week will usually make much slower progress than those who have time to ride more frequently. Co-ordination and balance can also be variable with the beginner.

- **Psychology of the rider.** Understanding what the mind is thinking is also relevant to the teacher. You need to know, for example, if the rider is nervous, confident, putting on a 'brave face', angry (with the horse or with you), or irritated by his own inadequacy. A rider with a poor attitude is not easy to teach. It is difficult, if not near impossible, to change a rider who firstly does not believe that you are right about their faults, and secondly does not think that they need to change. Fortunately that rarely happens with novice and beginner riders.

5 Planning Safe Lessons

AS A TEACHER (especially when dealing with children or beginner riders of any age), safety is one criterion that must come very near the top of any list of your responsibilities to your pupils. You, as the experienced qualified person in charge of your pupils, must take safety very seriously and ensure to the best of your ability that your pupils are never at risk through a situation to which you have exposed them.

Riding horses, however, is not without some element of risk, just as is any activity that we indulge in at any time of our lives. The teacher's responsibility is to minimise the potential risk involved in the riding activity while not detracting from the value or enjoyment of the sport. Safety is about awareness, so below we will consider how you can minimise the potential risks of riding as a leisure activity for weekly riders.

Facilities

- It is preferable and advisable to teach beginner and inexperienced riders in an enclosed area. This may be an indoor school or an outdoor school with an all-weather surface, or it may be in an enclosed paddock or a corner of a field which has been marked out for the purpose.

- There should be a policy within the riding school or set by the instructor in charge, that all horses/ponies are led to the school 'in hand', and then the ride all mount at the same time under supervision and with assistance if required. Similarly the return to the stable yard after a lesson ends should be similarly regulated, for safety.

- The riding area should be well maintained; any gate or door should be fully closed during the riding lesson.

- There should not be unnecessary equipment left lying haphazardly around the school during the riding lessons lest a horse or rider fall over it. (Jumps should be in use or stacked neatly in one pile on a three-quarter line in the school or brought in as needed from outside the school.)

- The facilities should be well maintained. This may not be your responsibility, but it should be a policy of the establishment.

Suitability of mount

Mounting your riders is a major consideration when dealing with any weekly riders, but particularly those who are in the early stages of learning to ride. An experience where they feel 'over horsed' by the animal, or in any other way feel uncomfortable, may put them off the sport before they have really become 'hooked'. They are not yet able to balance their developing knowledge and ability with the fact that some horses will be easier to ride than others. Try to use the following as guidelines in mounting your riders.

- Size of horse/pony appropriate to size of rider. Avoid putting a tiny rider on a big, scopey horse and vice versa.

- The horse should be easy to motivate forward, stop and turn left and right.

- The horse should not be very extravagant in its movement nor, conversely, as stiff as a board.

- The horse should be smooth in its reaction to the rider and also to possible outside influences. For example, a horse that spooks violently and shoots unexpectedly sideways with no warning, will prove to be a very disconcerting mount for a novice rider whose balance and co-ordination is not yet very good.

- A rider who feels comfortable will be more confident and this builds into increased competence.

- Riding a variety of horses is to be encouraged so that riders do not feel that they always want to ride their 'favourite' horse. This is by far the most practical arrangement to have in any commercial riding school. Otherwise everyone wants to ride the 'easiest' or most comfortable horses, and inevitably the most popular horses are all favoured at the same time.

Size of ride

The standard of the ride will to some degree dictate how many riders it is viable to have in one lesson, but also a more experienced instructor will be better able to control a large ride, particularly if the riders are of mixed ability, than will a less experienced teacher. The size of the facilities will also have some bearing on the size of the class. In theory, (commercially) the bigger the ride, the greater the profit margin, but safety may be compromised and this must never happen.

In an enclosed area with one competent instructor (experienced BHSAI or higher) then the author considers up to eight in a group to be workable. If you set the upper number at eight, often one or two riders do not attend due to other commitments, and the class lesson will regularly end up with a maximum of six; this is an easy number to deal with. Less than six riders and the lesson is commercially not very viable; more than eight riders becomes a good money earner for the establishment but it does not provide the riders with a good teaching environment – only the opportunity to follow a large group around with little time for individual riding.

Standard of ride

When one considers the size of a ride, one must also consider the standard of the riders. Experienced riders will take some responsibility for the way their horses go; however, novice/beginner riders need to have the constant support of the instructor because they are not yet able to help themselves very much.

It is much easier to teach a group of competent riders than to deal with a group of beginners who have no innate awareness of ... well, anything. It is also much easier to teach a group who are all of similar standard, than to have a wide range of abilities which must all be catered for in one group.

Standard of instructor

As with any employment or activity, the better qualified the person is, the better they do what they say they can do. (Within reason!) The more mature, experienced and qualified the person is, usually the more equipped they are to deal with the ups and downs that are likely to manifest themselves in any beginner or novice riders' class lesson.

Choice of work

The choice of work will always be the decision of the instructor and should always be designated as a result of:

- Assessing the riders (competence and psychology).

- Assessing the weather conditions (today it is cold, which may make the horses sharp; tomorrow it may be hot and humid and the horses may feel lazy).

- Assessing the facilities (e.g. how big is the school? is the surface wet/dry/heavy? how will it affect the way of going of the horses?).

- Staying within a subject range that you feel confident in. (For example, do not try to teach flying changes if you have never taught more than basic canter work with a novice horse.)

Do not allow your regard for maintaining safety to become so overwhelming in emphasis that you are inhibited in your development of work and then fail to improve your riders and teach them to ride effectively and with practicality. This in turn will make them over-safety-conscious and they may then lose or lack confidence.

You can progress the work and choose something more challenging:

- If you have assessed the partnerships as being confident (to a level).

- If you have seen them carrying out a particular task competently under instruction before (or a closely allied exercise, e.g. trot without stirrups and then canter without stirrups).

- If they have ridden the horse they are riding 'today' on a previous occasion and enjoyed it.

- If you have suggested an exercise, discussed it with your pupil(s) and they agree that they would like to work on it.

- If you have considered all the factors which might affect safety (weather conditions, heat/cold/rain/wind, spooky situation – plastic bags, heavy traffic close by).

Having considered all the criteria for maintaining safety then you must progress with a chosen exercise if you believe that it will improve the rider's expertise. For example, work the rider either without stirrups in trot or canter. By not progressing (in the interests of safety) you risk making the rider more tentative, more protected and therefore not able to ride so competently, so it becomes a 'vicious circle' where in trying to be safer you make the rider less capable, less self-sufficient and less able as a rider.

To summarise:

- The choice of work must always be relevant to the level and ability of the rider.

- The choice of work must always be within the capability of the teacher.

- The choice of work must be relevant to the physique and fitness of the rider and to a degree the fitness and ability of the horse.

- The choice of work must be comfortably in the range of teaching expertise of the instructor.

Dealing with parents and observers

It is inevitable, particularly when you are teaching children, that there will be people watching the lesson who have a personal involvement with the rider. These onlookers will probably fall into one of the following categories:

- Mother, father or both.

- Grandparent, sibling, other interested relatives.

- Friend of the rider.

- The person paying for the lesson, who may be any of the above or none, and if none then maybe a spouse, partner or boy/girlfriend.

For some reason, observers of riding lessons often think they have a right to influence the lesson, possibly because:

- They have paid for the lesson and therefore have some right to the input.

- They have a horse themselves, or have ridden thirty years ago, or have bred horses all their life, etc. etc. which gives them the right to dictate the progress of the lesson.

- They are a parent/friend/partner etc. and know better than you do what the rider wants to do in the lesson today.

I want to state very strongly here that you, as the instructor, have ultimate responsibility for how any lesson progresses or develops, and you can be accountable for any incident that might occur within it. If you surrender that responsibility (even if you are under some pressure from an observer to do so) and there is a problem within the lesson (e.g. a rider falls off and injures himself) YOU will be held accountable. If an incident occurs in spite of your every effort to conduct the lesson safely and progressively, then your professionalism remains intact. If, however, an incident occurs because you allowed your better judgement to be overruled by an observer, you would not be in a position to defend your actions.

While it can be difficult to learn how to be assertive yet polite to observers, you must **ALWAYS** maintain authority over your riders. You must never allow an observer to influence the choice of work for a lesson. That does not mean that you cannot listen to requests or discuss the possibility of specific work for a lesson, but it does mean that your judgement is always binding and final. Observers need to understand that your decision, as the instructor, is made always with the best interests of the rider primarily to the fore.

It can be helpful if observers are requested to abide by a code of conduct or set of rules, and that these rules are adhered to by everyone in the establishment. The following might be examples of what could be in place:

- Observers may watch only from a designated area (preferably warm, dry and undercover, and out of earshot of the riders).

- Observers may not communicate with any rider while a lesson is in progress.

- Observers may not vocalise their opinions of any rider while a lesson is in progress.

- Children, if watching with adults, must behave in a quiet, well-organised manner, which in no way could frighten or distract the horses/ponies.

Observers should feel able to discuss lessons with the instructor, or a senior member of staff as necessary, but should not be able to dictate terms such as:

- Which horse/pony 'their' pupil wants to ride.

- By whom they want 'their' pupil to be taught.

- Which lesson 'their' pupil will ride in.

- What work 'their' pupil will or will not do in the lesson (for example: 'My child will not ride without stirrups').

In this increasingly litigious world it can be difficult to set terms for every instance. From the author's experience, if the terms are set out and understood prior to commencement of lessons in the centre, then it is much easier to maintain authority. New clients either accept the rules of the establishment or go elsewhere.

6 Teaching Lunge and Lead-Rein Lessons

GIVING LEAD-REIN AND LUNGE LESSONS will be something that most instructors will be involved in on a regular basis if they are teaching in a commercial riding school, which inevitably will have teaching beginner and novice riders as a substantial part of its business. The instructor takes on a big responsibility in this aspect of his work because the early experiences of the pupil on the lunge or lead rein will set the seal on whether individuals decide that riding is a fun and enjoyable thing to do, or whether the activity is something that they decide is not for them after all. We will consider each lesson separately. Whether the riding school offers both lead-rein and lunge lessons to clients will depend on each school's policy.

Lunge lessons

Lunge lessons are one-to-one lessons where the instructor not only has the responsibility of teaching the rider but also must control the horse competently.

Lunge lessons have the following advantages:

- The rider is free to concentrate on himself, especially his position and balance.

- The rider can be introduced to the gaits and the sensations of riding, while the horse remains totally under the instructor's control.

- They allow the rider to develop a sense of confidence in the horse's movement before being able to ride independently.

- The instructor can clearly observe the rider at all times.

Giving a lunge lesson. Rider working without stirrups in trot.

- The instructor can establish a good rapport through body language and positioning in the circle, with both the horse and the rider.

The disadvantages may be listed as:

- Some riders do not feel confident about having the instructor at a 'remote' distance, i.e. at the end of a long rein.

- The rider may develop small faults on the outside of his body and these are not visible to the instructor from his position in the middle of the circle.

- If the horse is unsettled for any reason it may frighten the beginner rider before the instructor can bring the situation under control.

- A large amount of space is required for a 'one-to-one' lunge lesson, whereas several beginner riders could be taught together in a lesson taken by a competent instructor and several able leaders.

- Lunge lessons are labour-intensive on instructors, and physically demanding on horses.

Let us consider the skills required by the instructor to deliver a good lunge lesson and some of the requirements for teaching on the lunge.

Instructor skills and general lunge-lesson considerations

- The instructor must be able to lunge the horse effectively enough that a forward-going, consistent rhythm is maintained in the trot work.

- The horse must work on a circle that is large enough (at least 15m, and preferably nearer 20m) to enable the rider to maintain a better balance and not feel that they have to lean inwards, as with too small a circle. A large circle will also minimise the stresses exerted on the horse's limbs, which are exacerbated by a smaller circle.

- The instructor must be capable of maintaining the consistent activity of the horse while being observant to the needs of the rider and giving him relevant help and corrections.

- The instructor must be able to consistently 'read' the attitude of the horse throughout the lesson, and be aware of the horse becoming anxious or tense, lazy or tired before any of these affect the quality of the teaching given to the pupil.

- The instructor must be mindful of the quality of the way of going of the horse (working evenly on both reins and through transitions from one pace to another). This will ensure that the rider experiences the correct feeling of the horse, which will in turn help him when he comes to control the horse independently.

- The instructor must always work to achieve the best quality of work from the horse, both for the rider's developing feel and also, and most importantly, for the maintenance of the way of going and the athleticism of the school horse.

- The choice of work will be dictated by the level of ability of the rider, and it is essential that the instructor should assess the ability of the pupil before deciding on what work to develop.

- Because lunge lessons are so intensive for both horse and rider it is therefore essential that in a beginner or novice lesson of usually around 30 minutes, sufficient time is given to basic good principles such as mounting, loosening up the rider and working on position, so that these are secure and established as a basis for the rider developing independent riding.

The lunge horse

A horse that is suitable for giving lunge lessons to a rider is a well-trained, experienced, calm and obedient animal. Whatever the level of rider, the horse must work consistently in his paces, be secure to the contact and work evenly on both reins on a large circle (15m to 20m).

The horse suitable for the beginner or novice rider should have paces which are smooth and not extravagant, whereas the horse for the more competent rider can have bigger movement, which will test the rider's balance and co-ordination more.

Young horses (under five years of age) are not usually physically or mentally strong enough or established in their work to be appropriate as mounts for lungeing the rider.

Teaching a lead-rein lesson

Lead-rein lessons are more usually given to children, although in some instances adults may also request or benefit from a lesson on the lead rein (for example, a rider who is particularly nervous, or riders with disabilities).

There is the same element of the one-to-one (leader to pupil) relationship with the lead-rein lesson as with the lunge lesson, although the leader may not always be the instructor or teacher. In some riding schools, groups of beginner or novice riders may be taught together in one lesson, where each rider has his own competent leader but the overall control and teaching of the lesson is directed from the instructor (who is not leading anyone). This can work very satisfactorily and is less intensive for the riding school than a one-to-one instructor-to-pupil ratio.

The advantages of lead-rein lessons are:

- Some riders, particularly children or those of a more nervous disposition, feel more confident because of the close proximity of the handler.

- There is minimal risk of a horse becoming unsettled because the handler can deal with any such situation much more swiftly than when lungeing.

- A group of riders can effectively be taught together with one instructor and several leaders. In this situation riders can learn from each other and share their enjoyment and problems.

- Lead-rein lessons are less demanding on school riding space than lunge lessons.

The disadvantages of lead-rein lessons are:

- Some adults do not feel independent enough and want the 'freedom' offered by a lunge lesson.

- If the instructor is also the leader, his view of the rider is limited because he has to stay close to the horse's head.

Instructor skills for teaching a group of lead-rein riders

- The instructor must be able to supervise the group evenly and offer help to each rider as an individual at frequent times during the lesson.

- Control of the initial part of the lesson is essential, and the leaders must be capable of giving adequate support to their riders in leading the horse to the riding area, helping the riders to adjust girths and stirrups and then to mount.

- It is the instructor's responsibility to monitor the rider's basic position and make relevant corrections to improve it.

- The control of the lesson is vital to give each rider adequate opportunity to practise developing skills but also to allow them time to watch other riders from whom they will also be able to gain valuable learning.

- It is your responsibility to make sure that the riders are all equally worked, but that too much is not asked of them over and above their physical fitness and ability. Remember that most beginner or novice riders ride only once a week.

- Lead-rein lessons will usually last about 30 minutes and the content of the lesson will depend on the ability of the rider. Some guidelines for lesson content can be found in the BHS Learn to Ride book; see also the sample lesson plans at the back of the book.

General considerations when teaching lunge or lead-rein lessons

Usually these lessons are directed at less experienced, beginner or novice riders, except in the case of a more competent rider using a lunge lesson as a means of practising or improving their depth, security or feel as a rider.

- Always consider and maintain the confidence of the rider.

- Constantly monitor the rider's fitness and ability to fulfil the work you are expecting.

- Explain clearly whatever you are planning to do. For example, when making a transition from one pace to another give the rider clear information about how this will occur.

- If necessary make sure that the rider knows exactly when to use aids or influence the horse and when you (or the handler) will influence and assert control on the horse.

- Explain clearly the way aids should be applied. With a novice rider this cannot be done too often.

- Never assume knowledge or ability; always assess the rider on each occasion then choose and regulate work accordingly.

7 Teaching Children

T EACHING CHILDREN CAN BE CHALLENGING, fun and tremendously satisfying. It is helpful if you like children and can identify with them, but this is not essential. What is a must is that you should care deeply about ensuring that anyone you teach has as good an experience in their first introduction to riding horses as it is within your power to give them.

Special considerations

- Children have a limited concentration span – the younger the child, the shorter their attention span. In the author's opinion children under the age of five years can do little more than sit on a pony and develop feel for balance and co-ordination. Limited and slow progress may be made in formal riding lessons.

- It is essential that the riding lessons are fun and, within the parameters of safety, allow the children to express themselves, laugh, communicate with the pony, each other (if in a group) and with you, the instructor.

- Children who are keen to learn to ride of their own volition are rarely fearful: they are keen to start their newly chosen activity and have no reason to be afraid of what they have chosen to do.

- Fear arises from a previous bad experience, which imprints the anxiety on the child's memory. It is therefore a huge responsibility for the teacher to make sure that the children's experiences in their riding lessons are all as predictable and good as is possible.

- Children accept that there may be uncomfortable or less easy experiences, and

Child rider being led with a supporting hand from the leader, to assist balance and confidence.

these are taken in context as long as there has been some prior warning of them and much support offered for the child to be able to cope. For example, for the first canter lesson, adequate information should have been given that the canter is faster than trot, that going from trot to canter and back to trot again will be faster than anything they have felt to date, and that the rider should try to slide his or her seat in the canter to move with the pony and not try to 'rise' as in the trot. The child is then well prepared for what is to come.

Conversely if the child is suddenly confronted with something that is totally unexpected, for example the pony running off without any warning, then the child may feel apprehensive and anticipate further unpredictable happenings.

- Children enjoy learning in a group; they gain confidence from each other, they can encourage each other and laugh with and at each other. This can be a great way to develop learning.

- Remember also, however, that a bad experience within the group will need careful handling on your part to ensure that negative results are not forthcoming from the incident.

Teaching children with more experience

Developing the skill of the child rider can be immensely satisfying for the instructor and should be great fun for all concerned.

- Age should not be an inhibitor to progress.

- Progress should be dictated primarily by ability. Having said this, however, it is essential that if a child shows precocious talent in riding, attention is paid to securely establishing good basic principles of the rider's position, understanding of the aids and their application, and a true harmony and appreciation of riding as a partnership with the horse/pony.

- It is easy to be overtaken by the enthusiasm of finding a talented young rider who has a huge desire to learn as much as possible in a short period of time.

- There is no substitute for the steady accumulation of expertise through sufficient practice, and this is essential if the young rider is to have sustained ability at a higher level in the future.

- Within a group, if one child shows much more ability than others, the instructor has to be innovative to challenge the more able rider while not compromising the safety or overtaxing the less able members of the group. The more able rider should either be moved to a group of a higher ability to give him new challenges, or the individual should be taxed within the group by riding a more difficult horse/pony, or by riding a more demanding model of an exercise used for the whole group (for example, riders working without stirrups – less able stay in trot, more competent are asked to canter as well).

- Those with more experience in general should be given greater depth of theoretical knowledge to back up their practical learning. It is essential that riders become familiar with such subjects as the difference in paces, the sequence of the paces and how the horse's legs move in each pace, and what is meant by rhythm, balance, impulsion, suppleness, etc.

- Developing the skills of children with more experience may include introducing jumping, both over show jumps and cross country, team and individual games, hacking and bare-back riding. All these subjects will be covered in more detail in later chapters.

NOTE: There is a summary of the differences between teaching adults and children in the next chapter.

Child awareness and child protection training

Remember that your responsibility to the care and well-being of children is of paramount importance. In England and Wales a child is classified as anyone under the age of eighteen years of age. It is a requirement for all instructors registered by The British Horse Society on the official Register of Instructors to hold a certificate of attendance on a course identifying Child Awareness and Child Protection issues. This course will improve the awareness of those in charge of children during riding lessons and help them to identify such issues as fear in children, children experiencing bullying and perhaps children changing in behaviour due to outside influences at school, at home or in another environment away from their riding lessons. From 2004 it is likely that attendance on a Child Awareness course will become a mandatory requirement prior to candidates sitting The British Horse Society's Preliminary Teaching Test. Any instructor currently on the BHS Register of Instructors is required to attend a Child Protection course.

8 Teaching Adults

AN INSTRUCTOR WHO IS TRULY VERSATILE, and therefore very employable in a commercial riding school, will develop the ability to teach children and adults with equal competence, even though the two require quite different skills in many ways.

The subject of riding remains constant; however, the method through which that subject may be delivered will need often to be different.

Here are a few of the teaching considerations that adults may present:

- Adults, by their maturity, have a far greater awareness of the complexity of the subject and this may confer on them many anxieties, doubts and inhibitions. They are aware for example of

    - how far they are sitting away from the ground when mounted on the horse;

    - how fast the horse is potentially capable of going if they are not fully in control;

    - how little control they have due to their inexperience.

Factors such as these, plus others, may affect the adult's ability to react without fear and inhibition and to trust you, the instructor completely.

- Adults will have a far greater concentration span than children and may seek to be challenged beyond their practical or physical ability.

- Some adults will have studied the subject of riding and be very well versed in theoretical knowledge. They may develop frustrations in their lessons when their physical abilities are unable to match their theoretical knowledge.

- Adults may find the balance and co-ordination of riding a horse extremely challenging. A lack of physical fitness or a poor physique (e.g. being overweight) will again lead to frustration at a perceived lack of progress.

- Adults will often be frustrated by not progressing more quickly through the perceived stages of learning to ride. They may be anxious to canter and jump well before they are ready to embark on these activities.

- Maintaining adults' confidence and enthusiasm in you and in their newly chosen sport, while progressing the work at a rate by which competence will be well established and not fragile, is an art for you, the instructor, to work at.

- Adults often prefer the intensity of private lessons and the one-to-one attention that these offer. However, a class lesson may be more in the interests of the development of the rider, because of the benefits achieved by watching other people's problems and the reduced focus that several riders being taught together puts on each rider.

- Adults tend to be more assertive about the horses that they like and do not like to ride. They will often not be persuaded into seeing the benefits or challenges of riding a horse that they perceive as difficult or that they do not enjoy riding.

Teaching beginners and novices

It is important always to explore the reasons why an adult chooses to take up riding as a new sport. Unlike children there will usually be a clear reason for an adult wanting to start riding.

These may fall into the following categories:

- 'Always wanted to ride but never had the opportunity before due to lack of finance/ time/ opportunity.'

- 'My child has learned to ride, we want to get a horse/pony for her and I want to be involved and able to ride as well.'

- 'A close friend or partner rides and I want to be able to ride too.'

- 'We are going on a riding holiday with the kids this year and I want to know what I am doing.'

The first reason listed above is the strongest personal motivation for starting the sport; the other three are linked to another person's primary interest.

Beginner adults will need careful guidance as to how they may start their riding. Clear explanation should be given about lead-rein lessons, lunge lessons, and group versus private lessons. Encourage adults to watch a lesson so that they are completely familiar with the procedure before attending their own first lesson. This will give them time to analyse each area of the lesson and decide how they personally are going to deal with any aspect that they perceive as being difficult.

Make sure that each stage of each lesson is well consolidated before moving on to the next phase of difficulty. With the adult's greater degree of concentration, higher development of intelligence and reasoning power, it should be easy for you to find a range of ways of teaching the same lesson. In this way competence is assured through repetition and practice, but interest and enthusiasm are maintained before moving on to a new area of education.

Adults will often be extremely conscientious in studying the subject they are working on in any particular lesson. Often their theoretical knowledge of the subject may be more up to date and 'on the ball' than your own! If really keen, they may have studied the subject in virtually every book and any other source they can access, and this results in a greater intensity to achieve competence during their precious practical lesson with you. This can be an advantage if the increased knowledge of the subject enhances the rider's ability to carry through the practice. If, however, the increased knowledge inhibits the rider because their theoretical understanding actually impinges on their acceptance of their current level of practical ability, then your role as the instructor becomes even more critical. In this case your approach could be along the following lines:

- Be supportive of the commitment that your pupil has shown in studying the subject so thoroughly.

- Give time to discuss the theoretical aspects of the subject in relation to the lesson.

- Discuss, for example, the aids for movements or work and how they should applied.

- Emphasise the fact that while studying the subject is interesting, helpful and satisfying, there is no substitute for practice and that no amount of reading or studying will short-cut the learning needed from practice and repetition.

- Discuss the possibility of using such techniques as mental visualisation or rehearsal (refer to sports psychology theory), which can help convey familiarity and competence through mental repetition of a method (e.g. successfully riding a 20m circle in trot).

Teaching adults with more experience

As adult riders develop in confidence and competence they often tend to spend more time and money on the sport that is beginning to consume them in an all-encompassing way.

This is a very common occurrence where riding is concerned, and there is little difference here between children and adults who catch the 'riding bug' wholeheartedly. The main difference is that adults can and will dictate how much time and money they spend on their sport, and this can become ever-increasing.

Adults usually fall into two categories when they become 'hooked' on riding. Either they quickly choose to become first-time horse owners and fall headlong into the ownership category, or they continue to attend the riding school where they have learned to ride. In the latter case they require greater challenges to maintain their interest, satisfy their increasing passion and keep the financial benefit for you, the instructor.

If they choose the first option then you may need to consider what support they may need in purchasing their first horse and learning how to be a horse owner (this is beyond the remit of this book).

If they choose the second option then you will definitely need to consider every eventuality to keep your keen pupils motivated. Some of the following are possibilities:

- Encourage your pupils to have one of the school horses on a loan arrangement. They can treat the horse as their own, including paying for part of its keep, perhaps shoeing and the possibility of riding whenever they want to or for a designated number of sessions per week, including one or more lessons.

- Encourage your pupils to have one or more class lessons of varying types (perhaps one lesson on the flat and one jumping lesson).

- Encourage your pupils to take a private lesson as well as a class lesson to give individual help for the developing expertise and commitment.

- Encourage your pupils to compete in competitions run within the centre, and perhaps join a local riding club where they could use a school horse (or loan horse) for club activities.

- Encourage your pupils to start hacking and riding out in the countryside (depending on the surrounding area).

- Consider share arrangements with other livery owners in your centre.

The last suggestion can often be a very satisfactory solution for two adults with a similar passion for horses but with other commitments. Most adults who become 'horse mad' very swiftly find that, whatever their commitment to their equine friend, there are other major responsibilities which inevitably interfere with their new-found passion, be it a full-time job, a husband, children or ageing relatives, or a combination of several of these. Sharing the commitment with another like-minded horsey adult can be the answer, particularly if the two sharing have different job involvements and family responsibilities.

Other considerations when teaching adults

While children usually come to a lesson with a great deal of anticipation, enthusiasm and excitement (as long as they want to ride) and very little peripheral 'baggage', which can restrict the absorption of instruction, adults often come with many more 'hang-ups'. The following circumstances may inhibit your ability to teach your adult pupils effectively, but without giving your pupils a question-and-answer session on selected subjects before starting the lesson, you probably have no idea of the preoccupations they may bring to the lesson:

- Your pupil has had a row with a partner/child/parent/neighbour etc. before coming to ride.

- Your pupil has received bad news by post (e.g. financial problems or a relative ill) prior to coming to ride.

- Your pupil had a minor 'bump' in the car yesterday.

- Your pupil is worried about a partner's job/ children's exam results/ mother's impending doctor's appointment, and is thinking about any of these instead of your teaching.

- Your pupil is trying to fit in riding between going to the bank, doing the shopping and being in time to fetch the kids from school, but mustn't miss riding even though he/she hasn't time to do it justice.

All these examples highlight the mental state of mind that your pupil may bring to the lesson. You have to put the pupil gently into a state of mind to concentrate **ONLY** on their riding for the next 45 to 60 minutes. As an instructor of adults you must also be able to 'read' your pupil (see also page 27, understanding the rider).

When you teach a rider regularly, you develop an awareness of his overall personality and this should help you to be more aware of when he is having an 'off day'. It is important to be sensitive to the possible worries or problems of your pupils but not to invade their personal space. It is, however, also important that you teach as you find your pupil, and if a pupil's performance appears to be unusually poor during a lesson, it is vital that you explain to him why you will not progress on this particular occasion.

Some adults want to progress more than their confidence or nerve will actually allow. You need to decide whether by pushing them on a touch, they will feel challenged and satisfied because they are stretched a little beyond their normal 'comfort zone', or, conversely, whether that extra step will exert undue anxiety on them and have a detrimental effect. It is again your responsibility to discuss this with your pupil.

- When teaching adults you must always agree the terms of progress. If the rider does not agree the terms and does not share your confidence in the next step, then it should not be made.

- When teaching children you may need to take a decision on the next step forward in a lesson. This is because your pupils do not have the knowledge or understanding of the difficulty of the next step, nor whether they are capable of making it. Be absolutely sure that you can justify exactly why you chose to take the next step forward. If you cannot, or you are in doubt, then don't take that step.

Never be pressurised on lesson content or what a rider should be doing, by parents or outsiders who attempt to interfere and offer you advice.

Summary of the differences between teaching adults and children

In the role of the pupil:

- The child is dependent on the teacher.

- The teacher takes most of the responsibility for the learning process of a child.

- The adult is much more self-reliant and self-directing.

- The teacher's role is to develop and encourage this self-directed interest.

In the role of the pupil's experience:

- Children bring little if any past experience to the learning environment.

- Children depend on the instructor's input.

- New techniques must be introduced and taught to the child.

- Adults bring past experience accumulated over a lifetime in other circumstances and this can be a resource for learning for self and others.

- Adults attach more significance to what they experience than what they are told.

- With adults, while theory must be taught, most techniques are best learned from experience.

The readiness to learn:

- Children learn what they are taught to learn, to achieve parental or social approval.

- Children are motivated by a fear of failure, especially in comparison with their peers.

- Children are often taught in a group and the learning may be standardised for a similar age group and learning stage.

- Adults learn when they feel a need to take on the information.

- Adults may need the lesson to be adapted to meet the needs of the other demands in their life.

- Adults' needs and requirements for learning will be dictated more by their time and financial restraints.

9 Teaching Jumping

TEACHING JUMPING IS A SKILL IN ITS OWN RIGHT, and at higher levels may become an instructor's specialism. However, at a lower level, when working with riders in their early riding education, it is imperative that the instructor is both competent and enthusiastic about teaching jumping. For riders, learning to jump can open a door to more opportunities and fun in riding, as well as improving their sense of balance and feel.

When to introduce jump training

This can be a point for debate. Essentially, for a safe and positive introduction to jumping, the rider must be secure in walk, trot and canter, and able to ride confidently with and without stirrups in these paces. It is possible, however, to develop some security and confidence in the novice rider by introducing the concept of the jumping position. Through this you can encourage the rider to develop versatility in balance and position as a means to improving overall riding ability. The use of ground poles and manoeuvres can add interest and variation to the novice rider's lessons, but any actual jumping (i.e. leaving the ground) should wait until the rider's position and balance is sufficiently secure so as not to risk a set-back or fright.

Where to begin

Ideally, training the rider to jump should begin in an enclosed area (either an outdoor arena or indoor school). This should ensure that the footing is consistent and the horse thus able to maintain a smooth approach and departure, which minimises some of the responsibility put on the rider. There is some merit in riders learning to negotiate small natural obstacles (such as small ditches, logs, etc.) in the countryside, where they arise as barriers to the progress of a ride out hacking. In the author's opinion riders should still receive some preparatory training on how to adapt their position to be able to comfortably negotiate such obstacles in the open. (See learning to ride across country.)

Getting started

The instructor must have a very clear understanding of how the basic riding position for work on the flat can be adapted to the jumping position. (Note that whilst this text refers to the 'jumping position', the terms 'forward seat', 'poised position', 'half seat', and 'light seat' may be substituted.)

The instructor must clearly understand the following:

- The balance of the basic position for riding on the flat is dependent on the rider being positioned over the horse's centre of gravity when the horse is working in the basic gaits of walk, trot and canter. This position affords the rider balance and security when working on the flat and enables the horse to carry the rider's weight in such a way that he can do so with maximum ease and still develop and maintain fluent, elastic paces.

The basic position for riding on the flat.

Variations in the light seat.

■ The jumping position is based on the ability of the rider to be able to adapt his/her bodyweight through the three phases of the horse's jump and therefore allow the horse again to maximise his efficiency in balancing and carrying the rider while still jumping athletically.

As an instructor you must therefore be able to help the rider adopt the correct jumping position and then use work to achieve consistency in the rider maintaining that position, as his jumping experience grows.

　　When you decide to introduce work in jumping position, first demonstrate

Be willing to demonstrate the upright riding position (left) and the jumping position (right), from the ground.

Ask your pupils first to try adopting the jumping position in halt.

to your riders what the jumping position looks like and how they are best able to adapt their basic position to achieve it. You may need to:

- Consider whether the stirrup length needs to be adjusted. Often, for the novice rider, this is not essential as they may not be riding with very long stirrups anyway. It is up to you to recognise when the stirrup length should be gradually shortened to enable the rider to adopt a better jumping position.

- Discuss with the rider how he or she should go about achieving a more secure lower leg position with a greater breadth of base over the horse's back. By developing greater flexibility through the closed angles of the ankle and lower leg, the knee and thigh and the thigh and upper body, the rider will be able to vary the amount of weight distributed through the seat.

As the rider's competence and versatility in the jumping position develops, the ability to control the seat will also improve. Compare the dexterity of the upright position of, say, John Whitaker approaching a 5-foot show jump with the fragility of that of a novice rider approaching his first-ever jump.

Your role as the instructor is to:

- Teach the correct basic jumping position so that the rider is confident in his feel

Standing in the stirrups, in balance, in trot.

and ability to stay in balance with the horse when he (the rider) experiences his first jump.

- Make sure that the jumping position has been well practised on the flat, over poles and in many different exercises. The rider should then feel entirely confident in moving from the basic position to the jumping position and back again through walk, trot and canter before the first jump is introduced.

Cantering in jumping position.

An excellent exercise which tests the rider's balance over the lower leg is to ask pupils to stand up in their stirrups and find a perfect balance over the lower leg. At first they may need to hold on to the mane if they lose balance. Once they have found their balance they should be able to perform this exercise progressively through walk, trot and canter. This will set the riders in good stead for working to maintain balance when they start to jump.

Often insufficient time is spent establishing real security in the jumping position, and this in turn means that the rider loses confidence when jumping starts. When a rider starts to lose confidence in jumping then very quickly the horse follows suit and the situation becomes a vicious circle.

Novice riders must learn to jump on confident, genuine horses who maintain a calm approach to a fence and then jump easily and generously. If horses have to carry poorly balanced, nervous riders over jumps, then very soon they will lose their generosity as they persistently suffer because of their riders' lack of skill.

It is always the instructor's responsibility to make sure that the rider is as competent as possible for the level of work that is chosen. Horses must never suffer as a result of the incompetence of their riders.

Jumping in an outdoor arena or indoor school

The advantage of teaching jumping in an enclosed area with all-weather footing is that control of the horses is more assured and the going under foot will help to promote safety of both horse and rider. The size of the school, and whether you are teaching an individual or managing a number of riders in a group, will have some influence on how you develop a jumping lesson. Other factors include:

- The experience of your rider(s).

- The aims and aspirations of your rider(s).

- The number of riders you are teaching.

- The ability of the horses on which your rider(s) are mounted. (It would be unwise and unsafe to attempt to teach a jumping lesson with horses that do not jump or are capable only of trotting over poles on the ground.)

- Your experience in teaching jumping.

- The time allocated for the lesson concerned. Never start an area of jumping which you will not have time to finish or deal with if there are problems arising within the work.

When teaching jumping lessons the following guidelines may be helpful in choosing work for any level of rider.

- Always work well within your pupil's range of ability and experience.

- Always work your rider(s) on the flat in walk, trot and canter before commencing jumping. This will ensure that the horse (and rider) are suitably worked in and also give you the opportunity to observe the competence of both horse and rider and make any appropriate adjustments to the way of going, if this will ultimately help the jumping performance.

- Develop the jumping progressively and with a very clear pathway of jumping. This will ensure that, if at any stage there is a disruption in progress, either through confidence of horse or rider, it is very easy to move smoothly back a step to re-establish confidence before progressing again.

- Always manage the equipment safely. Often you will be working alone. Have the poles and stands somewhere they can be easily handled, but never in a position where they could accidentally cause injury to horse or rider. Make quite sure that

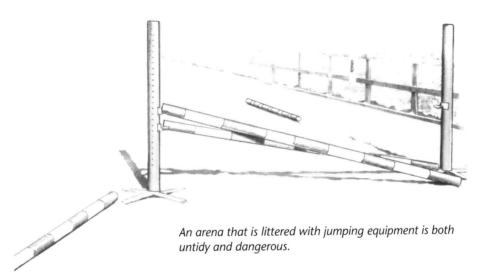

An arena that is littered with jumping equipment is both untidy and dangerous.

Jumping equipment neatly stacked in the centre of the school, ready for use as needed in a lesson.

loose equipment – poles, jump cups, etc. – is never left lying around creating a hazard.

- Always check and recheck distances between poles and fences. Be ready to make a quick adjustment to a distance (just rolling a pole in or out a few inches can make all the difference to the comfort and ease of the horse jumping). It is your responsibility to know when to move the distance, or when to adjust the rider's speed of approach, which can also help to make a distance ride more easily.

- When teaching a group of riders never allow riders to follow each other too closely over a fence. This is important because:

   (a) It can cause a horse to alter his way of going, because the second horse is influenced by the horse in front.

   (b) If a pole or distance is dislodged by one horse there is insufficient time to readjust the fence for the next horse, and this could cause an accident to the second horse and rider.

   (c) The rider of the following horse does not learn to influence his or her own horse in the approach, because of the close proximity of the horse in front.

- Make quite sure that you always see the approach, flight of the jump and the departure of every horse over every fence. This requires very good management from you as the instructor, but is essential if you are going to give a good jumping lesson. The effectiveness of your teaching will be based on your observations of the approach, jump and departure of every jump. Also, in the event of an incident, you will be certain that you saw everything that occurred during the jumping – and this is an important responsibility.

■ Good management of a jumping lesson comes with practice. You must be able to develop competence in moving riders around the jumping area. You need also to make them aware of their own safety and position with regard to other riders. This in turn prepares them for ultimate independent riding in a non-monitored situation (as will be required, for example, at a competition or horsey gathering).

■ It is important that you do not produce riders who can jump only if all the other riders are standing still. While jumping individually in a group lesson does occasionally have a place (see below) it is not a good method for maintaining fluency of the horse and rider's work, or for developing independence and rider awareness. Riders learn those skills only through practice.

■ There will be some argument on safety grounds for using the method whereby riders in a group stand still while one individual jumps. In the author's opinion, however, it does not ultimately prepare riders for safer riding. The method can be usefully employed in the short term: for beginner and novice riders; in the interests of giving both horses and riders a rest between jumping efforts; and for less experienced instructors who are still developing the skill of managing a number of riders on the move,

Jumping outdoors

Many of the factors that have been mentioned so far apply to teaching jumping lessons in general. There are, however, some points that have particular relevance to working outside.

■ It is likely that the working surface will be grass. When teaching less experienced riders on grass, remember that they will not have the necessary awareness or judgement of the variations in surface. It will therefore be up to you to advise and monitor them throughout your teaching to keep them working safely on the variable going.

■ It is your responsibility to notice whether the ground is hard (and to keep jumps smaller and jumping efforts limited to protect horses from jarring).

- If the ground is hard underneath but there has been recent rain, then the surface may be quite slippery with a hard resistance under the top few inches. This type of going can be treacherous, more so if riders are not competent at balancing their horses, especially around corners.

- If there has been excessive rain over a long period, the ground is likely to be deep, muddy and extremely 'holding' – i.e. heavy going. This can slow horses down, sapping their impulsion, and riders can then arrive at a jump with insufficient energy to negotiate the fence safely.

- Unrestricted space outdoors (without the safe perimeter of an indoor or outdoor school) can be quite daunting to less experienced riders who are not familiar with riding outside.

- It is your responsibility to ensure that your riders feel confident at all times outside.

- More instructions may be required initially to ensure that your riders do not stray too far. It is easy to describe markers, such as 'the tree past the gate' or 'where the ground starts to rise', so that riders learn to develop the use of the great outdoors while staying well within their comfort zone of feeling in control.

- Remember that horses nearly always behave in a communal way. If one horse gets 'full of himself' and starts 'running about out of control' then riders may quickly lose confidence and in no time several riders are showing signs of anxiety and loss of control.

- When teaching a ride outside, stay very aware and attentive, progress slowly but steadily, and ensure that the confidence of your riders is maintained because this will enhance the progression of the group.

- Weather conditions can influence an outdoor lesson. In a high wind the instructor's voice may not be heard, jumps may blow down, and the horses may be sharp, with 'the wind under their tails'. Cold, frosty weather may also make the horses feel more lively.

Cross-country riding and jumping

Riding across country requires a competent, secure and fairly brave rider. Some riders are naturally brave and will have a go at anything; others develop courage with competence – as ability increases so self-belief improves and they begin to feel that they are capable of more. This balance of competence and confidence is potentially fragile and easily upset through a bad experience. To the best of your ability you need to maintain that balance, progress it and protect it from a set-back – or, worse, an upset which could deliver such a blow to a rider's confidence that there is a temporary or permanent loss of nerve.

For riders with no previous experience, the development of cross-country riding should be from:

- The basis of a secure and confident jumping position (shorter stirrup, broader-based position, etc.).

- The progressive introduction of jumping, first in an indoor or outdoor school, then jumping outside.

- Hacking into the countryside will play its part in developing the security and competence of the rider.

- Learning to deal with varying types of going as described above and learning to ride up and down hills, and to negotiate gullies and banks, will all help to develop balance and versatility, which is vital to the competence of the cross-country rider.

- When the rider is developing increasing competence and enjoyment in jumping generally, then more specific work towards cross-country jumping can be introduced.

The most obvious differences between show jumping and cross-country jumping probably need little explanation. However, from the instructor's point of view, do not forget that your less experienced riders may need these differences explained.

- Show jumps are fences which are usually moveable and easily knocked down if hit by horse or rider. They are often highly coloured .

- Cross-country jumps are usually of much more solid construction, immovable, and often look wholly natural (i.e. part of the natural landscape – hedges, rails, ditches, logs, etc.). Generally, they do not move if hit.

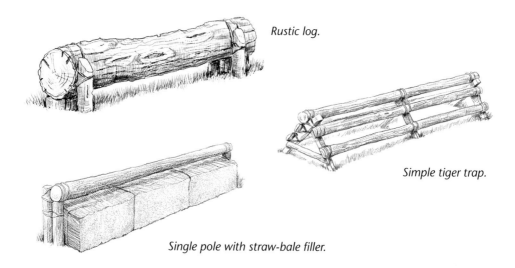

Rustic log.

Simple tiger trap.

Single pole with straw-bale filler.

- Show jumps require (from the rider) an ability based on good judgement of pace, rhythm and feel to the fence.

- Cross-country jumping requires similar skills but there must be an intrinsic ability to ride at a good pace (three-quarter speed). Learning to ride with developing pace in the canter work will take time and practice.

Introducing small cross-country type fences (such as those above) within the riders' jumping work will give them the feel for riding such obstacles. Small logs, ditches, and riding up and down hill, will all develop their feel and balance.

When teaching riders to jump cross-country fences, there must always be an emphasis on the greater speed required in the pace, while maintaining the balance, rhythm and control which is required in any riding and jumping.

Cross-country 'problem fences', such as corners, bounces, angled fences to name but a few, can be introduced to riders in a simulated indoor/outdoor situation. This will enable the rider to understand the concept of how to jump such obstacles without dealing with the complexity of the 'fixed' fence.

Finally, cross-country training courses are available for hire by individuals and/or groups (for schooling horses and riders) to give genuine course experience (or the ability to link fences together at a relevant pace) before a rider embarks on his or her first cross-country event or competition.

10 School Horses

GOOD SCHOOL HORSES ARE THE MOST AMAZING CREATURES and should be guaranteed a place of the highest honour when entering the pearly gates of horsey heaven! They can emanate from the most surprising sources, and it is your job as an instructor to recognise the developing or established 'perfect school horse' and nurture him to his final day.

Horses from the most varied of origins may become good school horses, and often they integrate well into the institutional life of a good riding school for the reasons given below.

- They enjoy a communal existence (whether stabled or at grass they are almost certainly in a group).

- They enjoy a very consistent routine.

- They are fed regularly and worked consistently and therefore are likely to maintain fitness and health.

- They are regularly shod, wormed and have their teeth maintained.

- They should maintain the quality of their work level if the work allocated to them is varied and they are ridden by competent as well as less experienced riders.

When the author ran a riding school it amazed her how often a horse owner would say, 'I don't want my horse/pony to go to a riding school!' In the author's experience there is no better place for a horse/pony to live. Many school horses live to a very great age in riding schools because they have all the advantages listed above.

Even horses that have been ridden exclusively by one rider can and do adapt fairly quickly to being ridden by a range of riders, some more competent than others. Some horses of a naturally sharper temperament will not accept less able or poorly balanced riders, but these horses can be used for the more experienced pupils in the school. Many horses adapt to giving exactly as much as is asked of them. These horses often become the exceptional school horses. They behave as quiet, reliable, docile creatures when being ridden by riders of limited competence. But when ridden by experienced riders these same horses raise their game and exhibit a range of work and movement only accessible to the more able rider. It is a pleasure to observe horses that are content in a riding school environment; they provide the backbone resource of any riding school – namely, the facility to teach riders at all levels. These horses are a priceless asset, and in many establishments are irreplaceable. So where can these gems be found?

Choosing school horses

It is impossible to write a formula for the perfect school horse – they come in all shapes, sizes, breeds, types and colours. There was a time when buying a coloured horse (piebald or skewbald) usually guaranteed a slightly lower price, which would be competitive to the riding school. This is a thing of the past, as coloured horses are increasingly popular and fashionable and now command higher prices.

Points to look for:

- **Size (height)**. This depends on whether you are buying for children or adults. Around 14hh would allow smaller and larger children to be mounted. If buying for adults and children, then a medium-sized horse up to 15.2hh could accommodate larger children, and adults who are not too tall or heavy.

- **Size (substance)**. A lightweight, fine-limbed animal will not be as versatile in his ability to carry varying size and weight of rider as will a horse with a little more bone and substance in his build.

- **Conformation**. It matters not at all if the horse is not stunning looking. If he is a little plain, say, with a roman nose, this will not affect his performance. Only avoid conformational faults which could affect the horse's ability to work consistently well or maintain soundness (e.g. weakness in limb alignment or poor action promoting interference).

- **Way of going**. Look for smooth paces which are neither too extravagant nor too limited and lazy. The horse should show some desire to go forward voluntarily without being too sharp and erratic.

- **Temperament**. The horse must be of a calm and amenable disposition. He must not become unsettled unnecessarily when riders are not perfectly balanced or predictable in their movement. School horses often develop an acceptance to varying balance in the rider, but it helps if they are generally unconcerned by it from the start.

- **Thriftiness**. The horse should be a good 'doer'. He should eat well and thrive, although this too is something that often develops as the horse becomes more secure in his environment.

You may find your school horses from some of the following sources. However, remember always to be on the look-out because school horses can turn up in the most unexpected circumstances.

- From a competition yard, when horses have come to the end of their competitive career.

- From a rider/owner who is giving up horses/going away to school/college/having a baby, etc. but wants the horse to go somewhere she knows it will be valued.

- From an advertisement in the local paper. In this case you must read between the lines regarding the horse's capabilities. It is unlikely that the advertiser will be looking for a riding-school home.

- From a sale. Here again you must use your experience and good judgement with regard to the description of the horse. 'Not a novice ride' may mean it is unridable by anyone except Lucifer himself; 'needs bringing on' may mean that it is barely backed and ridden away.

- From an establishment which is selling up and going out of business, or from a holiday centre such as a trekking yard selling stock in the off-season.

- From a reputable dealer who knows the type of horse you are looking for.

The last source can be one of the best. If you can establish a good relationship with a dealer who respects your custom, he will probably go out of his way to find horses that are suitable for your school. He will almost certainly take back any horse that does not work out for you as long as you are very straight with him over the reasons for its unsuitability. He will see you as a consistent, professional customer who understands his reason for business, just as he will respect and understand yours.

As previously stated, often the most difficult way to purchase a school horse is from private owners. Their perception of riding-school life may be stereotyped and false. They do not want their precious horse to be ridden day in day out by lots of different people and 'just do riding school work'. If you are trying to purchase a horse privately it may be helpful to take one of your more competent clients to try the horse, and then when the horse is well ridden (which is always encouraging to a vendor) suggest that the vendor comes to see your establishment to see just what a good life the horse would have if you decided to buy it.

Once purchased, it is important that the horse is gradually integrated into its new role. Even if it has been a fit competition horse it will not necessarily be 'fit' for the type of work that is demanded of a school horse. Later in this chapter we will consider fitness in more detail.

In the unlikely event that the horse does not settle happily into school work then you must identify this and deal with it. In the next section we will look at how to keep school horses happy in their work. However, if one horse is obviously not suited to the job, in spite of all efforts to maintain his morale, then you must be prepared to move him back into a private home.

Keeping school horses happy

It is of vital importance to the success of any riding school that the horses **are** happy. Only if they are happy will they work genuinely and be pleasant to be around. Your clients (and staff) are going to be less than satisfied if they are regularly met by bad-tempered, sullen horses who lay their ears back and are miserable whenever people are around them. What everyone should want to see are bright, alert horses with an enthusiasm for life. The whole yard should have an aura of interest and contentment emanating from the horses. Signs of contentment are as follows:

- The horse should be at the door or come forward in the stable when you come to the door to greet him.

- The horse's ears should be generally forward and 'kind'; he should not lay his ears back and make miserable faces at people around him. (He may, though, put his ears back occasionally if another horse invades his space.)

- While in their stables the horses should be resting quietly (but look interested if you disturb them).

- The horses may be eating hay, if it is in the stable.

- If tacked up waiting to be ridden, horses should not be standing in a dejected and 'tucked up' way.

- The stable and the yard as a whole should smell comfortably 'horsey' with no trace of a pervasive or unpleasant odour around it.

- When working, the horses should be genuine in their performance. The more forward-going horses will always be sharper, but all the horses should show some desire to work.

- When being handled and mounted, the horses should not be sour, grouchy and unco-operative.

Let us now consider how to maintain morale and happiness in school horses under the following headings:

- Feeding

- Fitness

- General care

- Living in or out

- Specialist care

Feeding

Part of the art of maintaining the mental and physical well-being of school horses is knowing how to feed them. Horses should be fed both for health and for the ability to sustain the work that is required of them. When school horses are required to work around two to three hours per day, albeit rarely consecutive hours of work, they need a diet which will give them a base contentment factor and the energy to carry out the level of lesson expected of them. Horses are herbivorous and their gut functions most effectively – and indeed they thrive best – when they are fed a diet which is high in fibre content. School horses, especially, will benefit from a diet which has a high bulk factor, such as is provided by good quality hay or haylage fed on a fairly ad lib basis. This provides them with the satisfaction derived from eating reasonably at will, which is as near to their natural behaviour as possible, even if they are not able to be turned out to grass regularly or for any sustained length of time.

In addition to the bulk basis of the ration, the concentrate feed should be adjusted to suit the type of work the horse is doing. School horses that are regularly working at higher levels during lessons and being ridden by competent riders, will need a higher energy input than horses ridden by novice or beginner riders. It is important to remember that the energy input of the feed must not make the horse sharp and unridable by the level of rider who will be most frequently mounted on him. It is your responsibility to monitor the work-versus-feeding regime of your school horses on an ongoing basis to ensure that the horses remain healthy, happy and safe mounts for all your pupils.

Fitness

School horses who work regularly for between two and three hours per day for between five and six days per week are fit – if fit is defined as the ability of the horse to do the work required of him. Your responsibility as an instructor in charge of school horses is to:

■ Monitor the way each horse copes with the work that is allocated to him.

■ Be aware of when a horse is a little 'full of himself' and therefore perhaps needing a little more work or a slight adjustment to his food rations.

■ Be aware when a horse is a little on the dull side and perhaps needs an upward adjustment of food or type of food, or maybe is working too hard.

■ Consider the age and previous work of the horse. Especially if a new horse is introduced to the school, it is important to assess how fit he is before putting him into a full regime of school work, which he may need time to develop fitness for.

Ex-competition horses and horses that have worked in a private yard need some weeks of conditioning to bring up their stamina for the broad-based type of fitness that is the foundation for a good school horse's working ability.

If a horse has had a period of time off for illness or injury, then he must be gradually reintroduced to his work (once completely recovered) so that he becomes stronger and the risk of a reoccurrence of the condition is reduced.

School horses work steadily hard, putting stress and strain on joints, tendons and ligaments. This is often due to the confinement of the areas in which they have to work, coupled with the added demands made by having to carry unbalanced, unco-ordinated and inexperienced riders.

It may be your responsibility to consider and monitor the fitness and way of going of school horses in your care. You must ensure that horses never work when there is any doubt as to their soundness and ability to fulfil work without any form of suffering to themselves.

School horses who are well monitored, whose work is allocated according to their fitness and appropriate to the level and ability of the rider, usually maintain well-being for many years and enjoy their working life to the mutual benefit of their contentment and your business success and reputation.

General care

Factors mentioned under this heading bring together the whole welfare and well-being issue of school horses. If the following are attended to on a regular and well-recorded basis then horses will thrive under your management.

- **Care of the feet**. Whether your school horses are shod or unshod (ponies who always work on a soft surface may be better off unshod), their feet need regular and consistent attention from a good farrier. Every horse should receive attention every four to six weeks, and your yard needs to apply a good system of daily checking plus the weekly preparation of a list of horses needing attention from the farrier. The establishment should employ a reliable farrier who attends regularly (every one to two weeks, depending on the size of the yard) and is available in the event of an emergency.

- **Worming**. Whether stabled or at grass, horses should be subjected to a well-judged system of worm control. The worming regime will vary according to each yard, the number of horses and how they are managed, but a good system of worm control helps to ensure healthy horses.

- **Clipping and trimming**. This will depend again on the circumstances of each individual establishment, how hard the horses work, how much they live in or out, what staff there are to manage them, etc. Horses should be kept tidy and well presented if the riding public are paying to enjoy riding as a sport. In winter it is best to keep manes pulled tidily, tails and heels trimmed, and to clip off some coat to enable the horses to work with greater comfort. Clipping should be done according to how much the horses are working and how hard is the work. Horses carrying largely beginner and novice riders will probably benefit from a trace clip or blanket clip, whereas horses working harder will probably require to have a more extensive clip. Remember that cold horses are unhappy horses, and are more likely to behave in an unpredictable way. Horses living predominantly at grass need the protection afforded by longer manes and shaggier heels and tails.

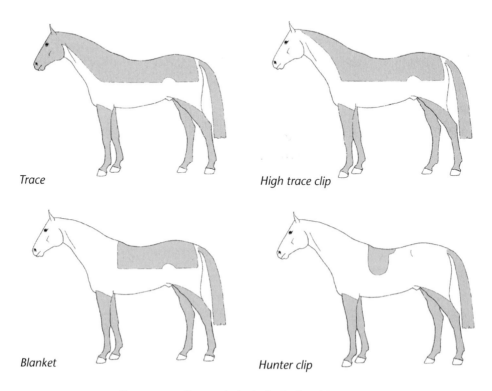

Trace

High trace clip

Blanket

Hunter clip

Choose your clip to suit the individual and his workload.

Living in (stabled) or out at grass

In general, stabled horses may be able to maintain a higher level of fitness than those living at grass because the whole regime of work-versus-feeding can be more easily monitored than when the horse is living out.

- School horses living out will often be calmer and less 'sharp' than stabled horses.

- Horses living out need greater protection from their coat and natural assets (mane, tail, heels) to afford protection from the weather.

- Stabled horses can be groomed more thoroughly than those living out, because the latter need the natural oils in their coat for protection from the elements.

- Stabled horses will be more costly to keep than those living at grass.

- Stabled horses are more labour-intensive in terms of care than horses living at grass.

- Horses living in a group at grass enjoy a more natural lifestyle than those stabled.

Additional care

In addition to maintaining your school horses in good health and keeping them happy, there are a few special points to consider:

- Horses should be closely monitored to ensure that they do not become over-weight (particularly in the spring).

- Being underweight is generally not a common problem, but nevertheless you must be able to monitor every horse's condition and ask yourself questions if a horse is suddenly losing condition.

- As school horses get older you must monitor their work carefully. As horses age, they are likely gradually to stiffen up, and in due course you may want to adjust or change their work from the more demanding work they were capable of when younger. Consider reducing lunge lessons, private jumping and cross-country lessons and more demanding private lessons. Allow the older horse to work more gently in group lessons of less intensity. As he gets older still, perhaps reduce the number of hours he can do per day or per week.

- Make sure that horses in summer or winter are rugged up accordingly. Weather can be very variable in spring and autumn so do monitor your horses carefully and make sure that they are always warm or cool enough.

- In summer make sure that horses do not suffer from the irritation of flies (at grass).

- In winter make sure that ice and cold do not cause your horses unnecessary discomfort.

11 Dealing with Problems

TEACHING WILL NEVER BE WITHOUT ITS PITFALLS. We will now consider some of the circumstances which can adversely affect the progress of a lesson and how these factors can be minimised by your good management and judgement as a teacher.

Nervous riders

At some time in our lives we all suffer from 'nerves', to a greater or lesser extent.

'Nerves' can affect different people in different ways and it is your responsibility as an instructor to be able to assess the nervous state of your pupils and make a judgement as to how much their nerves are affecting (or likely to affect) their performance in your lesson. Some riders may be unaware that 'nerves' are inhibiting their riding ability. Others over-focus on their fears at the expense of their ability to progress. Careful and tactful management of nervous riders is a skill that you must develop if you are to ensure safe progression of your lesson and development of your riders' confidence.

Some of the signs of nerves may be:

- Reluctance to do something a little more challenging within the lesson (e.g. attempt canter or start to jump).

- Reluctance to try anything outside their own 'comfort zone', the area that they feel totally confident about.

- Reluctance to ride certain horses/ponies that they perceive they cannot manage.

- Reluctance to do anything 'first', always preferring to see someone else take up the challenge before they do.

- Talking excessively (to hide nerves).

- Becoming quiet and withdrawn (also to hide nervousness).

- Becoming rather abrupt or quick in the way they react, instead of making smooth aid application actions; even verging on being rough and unco-ordinated.

When dealing with nervousness it is important to be sympathetic, supportive, but firm as well. Frequently a rider is looking for your assertion that he is capable of doing something he is nervous about, and if you are over-sympathetic then you may inhibit his progress, because he was just seeking your support. This is where your ability to 'read' the situation is so vital. Good communication is also important so that your pupil feels able to confide his worries in you and seek your advice. Remember that nervousness can be infectious within a group of riders. If one pupil shows a reluctance to do something, you may quickly find that the whole group follows the leader into a negative outlook. Again, it is up to you to prevent the nervousness of one individual from permeating the whole group, and therefore causing a negative attitude within the ride.

Stiffness

Stiffness in horse or rider is limiting and destructive. Since horse and rider are aiming to work in harmony, both bodies need to work at being relaxed, supple and elastic. Suppleness in horse and rider is something that should be a constant aim within any lesson. At the higher levels of equitation, where the rider may be looking to train or compete horses in dressage, suppleness becomes an essential criterion.

For the purposes of this text we shall consider stiffness of the rider. People vary greatly in their natural movement. If you watch your pupils in their normal activities off the horse (e.g. getting out of the car, walking into the yard) there will be small differences in their basic flexibility and natural suppleness. The mental state of the rider ('nerves', as previously discussed) also has a physical effect on the body, and thus your pupil may come to the lesson tense, nervous and therefore with increased stiffness, or relaxed, 'laid back' and supple.

Let us, for example, consider a rider who is rather angular and stiff in her natural deportment. What will your approach be to help her to be looser and less stiff when she rides?

- Make sure that she feels as relaxed as possible about her impending lesson.

- Ensure that someone is around in the yard to greet her on arrival and assist her in helping to find the horse she is to ride.

- Consider suggesting some unmounted exercises.

- Make sure that she is mounted well within her riding capability.

- Try to ensure that the environment in which she is to ride is familiar (e.g. a lesson she has been in before; someone else she knows is riding in the group; if new to the group she has been introduced to others).

- Aim the work towards gradually loosening up the riders, with exercises to help suppleness.

- Choose work that is easy for both horse and rider to enable the rider to feel at ease with what she is doing and therefore avoid stiffening in a situation which is beyond her control.

- Regulated work without stirrups may help reduce stiffness, as may individual lunge lessons to help the rider focus on her own position and 'feel' for the horse.

Stiffness can cause a loss of harmony with the horse and the partnership becomes anxious as a result, with co-ordination and balance being compromised.

Poor co-ordination

Good co-ordination is an asset to a rider because communication with the horse is dependent on the clear application of aids. We vary greatly in our natural co-ordination. A simple exercise to test co-ordination is to ask a person to use both hands at the same time, but with each hand carrying out a slightly different task:

- one hand pats the top of the head while the other hand makes a circular, rubbing motion around the tummy region; or,

Co-ordination test 1: one hand pats the top of the head while the other hand makes a circular, rubbing motion around the tummy region

Co-ordination test 2: one arm makes large circular movements backwards while the other arm makes the same circular movement forwards

■ one arm makes large circular movements backwards while the other arm makes the same circular movement forwards.

If co-ordination is not great then the rider is going to find it more difficult to use one hand to tell the horse one thing while one leg tells him something else. Controlling the horse always requires that the rider's hands and legs work in co-ordination, while each is giving a slightly different aid (e.g. aids for canter: inside leg on the girth for impulsion, outside leg behind the girth for controlling the quarters, inside rein creates a little bend for the direction and outside rein controls the speed and degree of bend). It is the instructor's responsibility to assess each rider's co-ordination and work to improve it.

These are some of the areas where an instructor may need to be specially aware of rider co-ordination.

■ **Basic position**. Look for consistency in the rider's position on both reins – often the rider may be better in one direction than the other. It is important to work on

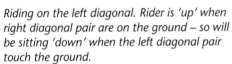

Riding on the left diagonal. Rider is 'up' when right diagonal pair are on the ground – so will be sitting 'down' when the left diagonal pair touch the ground.

Sitting on the left diagonal. As the left shoulder comes back, the foot is on the ground.

the side where the rider finds it more difficult to maintain correct balance and security before a crookedness or stiffness becomes established.

- **Aid application**. Watch for the way in which the aids are applied on both reins. The rider may show a 'stronger' influence with one hand or leg at the expense of the weaker side, which means that if they ride the same horse all the time (perhaps their own) they can make the horse 'one-sided'.

- **Diagonals in trot**. Some riders find it much easier to establish the correct diagonal on one rein than the other. It is important that the rider is not allowed to develop a feeling for an 'easy' diagonal and then to favour that one. Again, this would tend to make the horse one-sided (although this is more likely to happen with privately owned horses than it is with school horses).

- **Canter leads**. Novice riders who ride well-trained school horses are more likely to develop good positions, balance and co-ordination than those who rely on self-help when riding their own horse. Often the latter is not as well schooled, nor so accepting of the novice rider's inevitable weaknesses. This often shows itself in canter – the horse may develop an 'easy' rein, and a stiffer rein on which he may be reluctant to take the 'correct' leading leg.

Working on the rider's co-ordination is a vital part of training them to improve balance, feel and effect on the horse.

Exercises with and without stirrups, both on the lunge and within a class lesson, will improve co-ordination, as will encouraging riders to focus on how they prepare the horse and how they apply the aids. Careful attention to the rider's position and effect will ensure a progressive development of the rider's balance, security and competence, which will bring confidence and a sense of achievement.

Poor balance

As with co-ordination, some people are naturally much more balanced than others. You have only to look at small children in the early stages of learning to run about and play – some appear never to fall over, possessing an innate sense of self-preservation, while others seem constantly to be tripping over, grazing their hands and knees. When a person with poor natural balance takes up riding then the problem is compounded: their lack of control over their own balance is combined with a requirement to find balance on top of a moving horse. Not surprisingly, there can be quite a lot of issues to overcome.

As an instructor it is necessary to be able to recognise poor natural balance in a rider. Often a lack of balance is linked to stiffness; although it may also be linked to poor co-ordination. However, it is quite possible to find good balance hand in hand with poor co-ordination, and conversely, a lack of balance coupled with good co-ordination. Stiffness often creeps in with poor balance because the rider strives to achieve better security by 'clinging on' rather than through improved balance.

Recognising poor balance:

- The rider may find it difficult to know when his stirrups are level; he may be content to ride 'unlevel' and therefore develop a crooked or unbalanced basic position.

- The rider may find it difficult to 'follow the movement' in the basic stages of stopping and starting and turning.

- It may take the rider a long time to develop the 'feel' and balance of rising trot and canter.

- The rider may find any work without stirrups quite difficult.

- The rider may find some horses (the smooth, broad, easy-to-sit-on types) easier to balance on than others. It may be wise to develop your less-balanced rider's ability on these horses.

- The rider may find it difficult to adapt his position when learning the 'jumping position' and then acquire balance over jumps.

In being aware of poor balance, you are half way to being able to help your pupil(s).

Your choice of work and exercises must take into account the limitation of your less-balanced riders. Where, for example, you might work in canter without stirrups for some riders, with your less-balanced riders it would be wise to give them back their stirrups for this work, rather than risk a fall. Progress may be slower with riders possessing less natural balance, but safety and the confidence and well-being of the rider are always of paramount importance.

Loss of nerve

'Losing one's nerve' as a rider is something that can occur quite suddenly and irrationally (with no apparent trigger point), or it can creep up gradually, with the rider and the instructor being unaware of the tell-tale signs.

Sometimes riders who have demonstrated confidence and enthusiasm for riding can suddenly be radically affected by an incident (which often isn't major) and start to focus on all the negative aspects of riding (e.g. being out of control, falling off and hurting oneself). On other occasions loss-of-nerve symptoms may be set off by a trigger such as:

- Taking a break from riding after an injury, which may not necessarily be horse-related.

- Taking a break from riding to have a baby.

- Having a bad fall involving a broken limb, which inevitably conveys some weakness, period off work and sport and rehabilitation.

- Seeing a friend or loved one experience a fall and/or injury.

Symptoms of loss of nerve may be hidden by the sufferer for a while because they are embarrassed to admit them. These symptoms may include:

- Reluctance to take on new tasks or ride new or different horses.

- Reluctance to, say, canter or jump, or whatever it is they perceive as fearful.

- Making excuses for why they cannot do any of the above.

- Giving up riding altogether often with very little prior warning.

It is up to you, as their instructor, to reassure your pupil(s) that:

- 'Loss of nerve' is nothing to be ashamed of or to apologise for.

- 'Loss of nerve' is something that can and does happen, and that they are not unique, stupid or inadequate because they have suddenly lost their passion for riding.

- It is perfectly acceptable to take a step back from riding, and perhaps, when circumstances change, they will show a desire to want to try again.

- It is OK if they do not want to move on to jumping/hacking/whatever. They can stay at a basic level, well within their 'comfort zone', for as long as they want to.

- Everyone's aspirations are different, and that it is both acceptable and positive to be able to state what theirs are. They should not be influenced by others around them.

- They must never feel pressurised by anyone else (friend, parent, spouse, instructor) to attempt something that they have neither the enthusiasm nor the confidence to do.

Incidents and accidents

An incident can be defined as 'an event', 'an occurrence' or 'an episode'; whereas an accident can be defined as 'an event without apparent cause', 'an unexpected event', 'an unintentional act' or 'a mishap'.

Both incidents and accidents are an unavoidable part of life and certainly an occupational hazard of being around horses, whether handling them or riding them. It is therefore important that you, as an instructor, are able to deal with an 'unexpected event' with as much tact, sympathy and efficiency as the circumstances dictate.

As a professional, it is vital that you take every care to ensure that your pupils are never put at unnecessary risk through poor judgement on your part. Here are some examples of how this might be put into practice:

- Riders must always be mounted well within their capability.

- Riders must clearly understand any work or exercise that they are asked to carry out and must share responsibility for doing it (e.g. agree to work without stirrups or to jump).

- The instructor must be responsible equally for all members of a ride (e.g. if one rider is carrying out an individual exercise, the rest of the ride must still be under the eye and control of the instructor).

- The work must always be relevant to the assessment of the rider(s) on that day and not based on what they did last week or have told you they can do or have done before!

- If in doubt, don't do it.

- You can do far more with a rider you know, on a horse you know, in a school or environment that you are familiar with, than you will with a new horse and/or rider whom you have never taught before or in circumstances (e.g. very windy day, or much outside distraction) which may contribute to potential risk.

In the event of an incident or accident within a lesson:

- Halt the rest of the ride.

- Go to the casualty.

- Try to assess the situation which is evolving (loose horse, rider lying on the floor, sitting down, getting back up, etc.)

- Maintain an aura of calmness, sending someone responsible to get help, if deemed necessary.

- Always assist the potentially injured person primarily, while giving instructions to the rest of the group to maintain their safety and confidence.

Each incident or accident will produce a different set of circumstances that need to be dealt with accordingly. In general terms, however, it is your responsibility to:

- Deal with the occurrence, taking into account the safety and welfare of the person(s) involved and the horse(s) involved.

- Inform a parent if a child has been involved.

- Inform any relevant party if a rider has received injury requiring paramedical or hospital treatment.

- Make a thorough record of the incident, including any Health and Safety reporting under the regulations imposed by COSHH (Control of Substances Hazardous to Health or RIDDOR (Reporting of Incidents, Diseases and Dangerous Occurrences Regulations).

In the longer term it is your responsibility to consider why an incident may have arisen. Any incident, however minor, should have some kind of review process to consider whether the situation could have been avoided.

Any horse that has been involved in an accident may need some 'rehabilitation' to ensure that his confidence is not affected, which could compromise the well-being of his next rider. Minor incidents should be of little or no consequence, but, for example, if a horse received a bad fright from a large vehicle on the road then the next time such a situation arises the horse may revert to his 'flight' instinct and try to run away from the source of his fear.

Similarly, some record should be maintained to ensure that the next instructor of a rider who has had a frightening experience (perhaps their first fall) is aware of the background and is able to 'read' the confidence of the pupil and aim to rebuild any loss of nerve.

12 Teaching Games, Pony Club and Riding Clubs

Games

Teaching through games on horses/ponies is great fun and can be very educational, not only for children but also for adults.

Games, whether run for teams or individuals, can be stimulating and motivating. They teach the developing rider to think for himself and react automatically to the circumstances, without waiting to be 'taught' or told what to do.

In a group situation it is easy to develop the concept of learning through games by using exercises which test riders with a degree of competitiveness.

'Let's see who can do this' sets down a challenge to motivate riders to try harder. 'Let's see who does this best' uses the same concept.

Most exercises and games can be used for children and adults, except some of the more athletic type exercises, which should be used with caution for adult riders – you do not want them to go home with pulled muscles because you asked them to attempt contortions!

Examples of exercises and games which can be used for riders are given below. These can be adapted into team games if required, with two teams of three or four riders 'competing' against each other.

- Dismount on the offside and run around to remount on the nearside.

- Same exercise in reverse. Dismount nearside, remount offside.

- 'Round the world', as a race, first to complete. (See illustrations overleaf.)

- Walk and trot race. Trot up to a cone at the top of the school, walk back.

- Trot and canter race. As above, but canter up, trot back.

'Round the world'. The horse/pony must always be held for this exercise.

- Two poles spaced apart – 'Who can get the most trot strides between the two poles?'

- As above, but 'Who can get the fewest trot strides between the poles?' (Both these exercises can be done in walk.)

- Ride and lead. Trot or canter to cone, dismount, reins over head and lead back (run).

- Lead up to the cone, mount and ride back.

- Baton race. Members of each team at both ends – one rides up and gives a baton (whip) to the next rider, who rides back; this continues up and down until all riders have completed.

- Ride around the outside of the school and when a whistle is blown (or the instructor calls 'now') all ride into the middle of the school where they claim either a jump stand or a cone. Riders are eliminated if they do not get a jump stand/cone. The number of cones/stands is reduced one by one until there is an outright winner.

There are any number of additional games which can be set up for summer 'fun days' for children or holiday riders all of which develop confidence and independence. Both ponies/horses and riders alike enjoy the fun.

Pony Club and Riding Clubs

These organisations are prolific in most areas of the country. Pony Clubs cater for juvenile riders up to the age of twenty-five, while Riding Clubs tend to be for adults (although some Riding Clubs also have a very active junior section).

Instructors are always much in demand for instructional 'rallies or clinics', particularly during school holidays (especially for Pony Club) and in summer evenings. While most of the points already made in this book will be relevant, it is important for you to remember the following when teaching at Riding Club or Pony Club clinics.

- You are a 'visiting instructor' and as such will often not know the pupils you will teach.

- You will be teaching in a less familiar situation than normal and this may also not be as 'custom made' as your riding school 'at home'. You may be teaching on grass in a field instead of in an indoor or outdoor school. You must therefore take into account the influence of outside distractions and the possible effect of muddy or slippery conditions due to the grass footing.

- Your pupils may be apprehensive if they do not know you. They will probably be anxious to do their best for you, but may also be worried about whether you will like them or their horse/pony.

- Your pupils may not be 'on your wavelength' immediately. They must learn to 'follow' your way of teaching and understand your individuality.

- You may have to teach riders whose horses are less well-schooled and less predictable than your familiar school horses.

- You may not have access to the 'props' that you normally use in lessons (jumps, cones, etc.).

- You may need to consider the fitness of your horses and/or riders.

All these considerations must be in your mind as you assess your pupils, discuss with them their hopes and aims for the lesson and then decide on your programme of work.

You must be prepared, as always, to be adaptable in the work and make sure that you are constantly monitoring the progress, level of understanding, and confidence of your pupils.

Example Lesson Plans
for Classes on the Flat and Jumping

THE AIM OF THE FOLLOWING PLANS is to provide instructors with some practical ideas for class lessons. It must be emphasised that the instructor must always assess the riders on the day and choose work that is appropriate to how the riders and horses are performing.

The lesson plans, with their choice of options and faults to look for, should be particularly helpful to young or less experienced instructors who are learning how to develop their lessons. Through this work they will expand their observation skills and begin to be genuinely capable of helping riders overcome faults and problems.

The plans are not presented in order of difficulty, but are a random selection of the teaching scenarios that may be encountered in almost any riding school.

If, when reading any of the lesson plans, you are tempted to think, 'Why not do so and so?' please remember that these are just examples. In fact, they are 'my' lesson plans, which I have used on countless occasions when teaching groups of riders. Remember that any lesson may have an unexpected outcome, especially if you fail to control the horses and riders effectively.

I would stress again that, however predictable your class, you must **always** be prepared to adapt your teaching to what is actually happening and not stick rigidly to whatever you had planned.

In all the lesson plans we will assume that all the riders are mounted, stirrups adjusted and girths checked, so the lesson can commence.

Lesson Plan 1
Eight riders, mixed abilities, mixed ages

EIGHT RIDERS OF MIXED ABILITY, BUT ALL CAPABLE OF WALK, TROT AND CANTER WITH VARYING COMPETENCE. SOME ARE MOUNTED ON PONIES AND SOME ON HORSES. YOU HAVE ADULTS AND SOME CHILDREN, WITH THE YOUNGEST RIDER ABOUT TWELVE YEARS OLD.

The following lesson plan would give you plenty of work to cover in a lesson lasting approximately one hour. At various stages of the lesson there are options giving you a choice of exercise, so you should be able to produce several different lessons from this one basic plan.

If your riders are mounted on school horses/ponies (in a riding school) then you probably have the advantage that:

- You will know all the horses/ponies.

- The horses/ponies are more likely to be sensible and calm.

If your riders are mounted on their own horses/ponies (say, at a riding club clinic) then there will probably be more than one horse that is fractious, tense and 'running around', not much in control.

Very early in the lesson, aim to identify strengths and weaknesses. For example:

Strengths

- Everyone (it is hoped) shows some basic control.

- Everyone is keen to start work.

Weaknesses

■ Riders anxious with anticipation.

■ Some horses are unruly, which adds to tension in the rider.

■ Poor positions.

■ The rider is using excessive body movement, which is then often in opposition to their horse.

Getting started

■ The ride are all mounted, with stirrups and girths adjusted and checked.

■ In halt, and with the group lined up safely, speak to the riders individually.

■ Find out the riders' names. If you are not good at remembering names use a small notebook or card to record the first name of each rider and then some identifying feature of horse or rider which will give you instant recall of them. For example: 'Angela' – red girth; or 'Peter' – grey horse, overreach boots. You show much more involvement with your pupils and commitment to them if you find out their names rather than call out 'you, on the grey horse!'

■ Find out about the horse. If it is the rider's own, ask: How old is he? How long have you had him? What do you want to do with him? etc.

■ Ask if there is anything anyone particularly wants to do? It is preferable to try to build in something that your pupils are actually keen to do, provided that the request is reasonable and within the capability of the group.

■ Give a brief aim for the lesson (building in the request as mentioned above), e.g. 'We are going to try to establish calmness, harmony and control with your horses/ponies.'

■ Ask if everyone is familiar with riding in 'open order' (see facing page) . If you are met with a lot of blank faces then carefully and clearly advise them on how to ride in open order. If in doubt, or with a group you have never taught before, the best way to introduce this is to allow the riders to work in on one rein only. When everyone has moved around the school in walk and trot, change the rein and continue the same work on the other rein.

- Throughout this work be aware that basic softness, harmony and rhythm are the most important aspects of this working-in time.

Easy ways to direct work in open order

- Start everyone on the same rein in walk.

- Explain the principle that the aim is to stay in a space at all times, never getting too close to another rider.

- If one horse gets too close, its rider may have to slow down or halt to create space. It is your responsibility, as instructor, to advise and further assist the riders in how to stay away from each other.

The benefits of working in open order are:

- It enables riders to begin to influence the horse on their own, but if they are used to being organised in a closed-order ride, they may find their new-found independence less than easy at first.

- It develops the rider's sense of awareness of other riders close by.

- It develops the rider's efficiency and co-ordination to be able to influence the horse, irrespective of where the other riders are.

- It teaches the rider self-control and patience.

- It teaches the rider to think ahead and to apply aids in a well-prepared manner.

So having established the basic principles of working in open order (on one rein) you can introduce a basic theme of work.

For example (this is the basic description of what you want the ride to do):

'Working in trot, we are going to ride 20m circles at A and C and make transitions to walk over the centre line.'

More detailed information would be:

'You may ride a circle at A or C whenever you wish, but particularly if there is space to do so with no one directly in front of you. When aiming for a transi-

tion make a right-angled turn off the side of the school from the MBF side towards the HEK side, ride a transition to walk for a few strides over the centre line and then move up into trot again before making a second turn back onto the track on the same rein.'

Allow the ride to begin the exercise and watch them make some of the turns and circles. Be observant and prepared to correct any of the following faults:

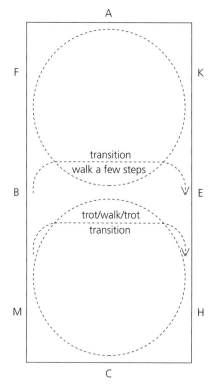

- Poorly shaped circles or poorly ridden turns. (Check the rider's knowledge of the aids for riding turns and circles. Look at the way the rider prepares for riding the turn or circle.)

- Loss of balance or impulsion or bend or rhythm through the turn or circle. (Check the rider's understanding of all these criteria and work to improve each or all.)

- Loss of rider's balance and position through the turn or circle.

After working on these movements for some time, and when the riders are showing greater consistency in their work, you could take up one of the following options:

Option (a) – Change the rein and continue the same work on the other rein;

Option (b) – Include work on the other rein, allowing riders to ride on both reins, changing the rein when they choose; or

Option (c) – Change the exercise.

We will choose **option (c)**, and you might explain it to the class thus:

'Now we will introduce some work on two circles with half the ride at one end

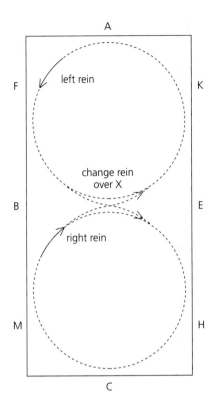

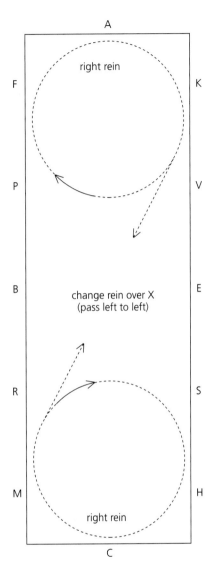

of the school and half the ride at the other end. We will have a left-handed circle at A, and a right-handed circle at C.'

Circles should be on opposite reins for safety (see diagram left), unless the school is 20 x 60m, in which case it can be safe to have two circles working in the same direction. So, in 20 x 60m arenas, with both circles on the same rein (as illustrated right), each ride would change the rein to circle at the opposite end, at the same time. That is to say, riders from A change the rein over X and circle at C; and riders at C change the rein over X and circle at A; and the rides pass each other left to left as they change the rein over X.

'Four riders in open order at A (on the left rein), four riders at C (on the right rein). Space out and maintain open order. Circle away within the circle if you

get too close to another rider. You may change the rein whenever you want to by crossing over X and taking the other circle on the new rein. If one person changes from A to C then one person must change from C to A, so that at any time there are always four riders at each end.'

Having done that, you could now consider working on the following options:

Option (d) – Transitions walk–trot, trot–walk;

Option (e) – Shortening the trot strides a little (keeping energy in the steps) and then lengthening the steps a little (without hurrying); or

Option (f) – Decreasing the size of the circle by spiralling down to 10m and then spiralling back out, still with the horse on one track (hind legs following the front legs). (See illustration below.)

Watch for any of the following:

In **option (d)** – look for similar faults or problems as were seen in the turns and transitions over the centre line.

In **option (e)** – look for the rider using too much rein (which merely slows the horse down while losing energy). The rider must make the horse's steps rounder and more elevated, so that as they cover less ground (shorten), the energy is not lost. Instead it is contained, producing a horse that is more 'coiled up' in a shorter, livelier frame.

In **option (f)** – look for the rider bringing the circle in progressively while maintaining the rhythm, balance, bend and impulsion of the horse.

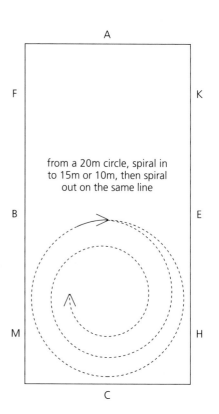

from a 20m circle, spiral in to 15m or 10m, then spiral out on the same line

There must not be an increase in bend in the head and neck only: the whole body must be involved from an energetic inside hind leg. When increasing the circle, keep the rider aware of the hind legs following the front legs.

Make sure that the riders take responsibility for working on both reins; encourage them to start changing the rein without your having to keep telling them.

After some work on any or all of these options you may decide it is time to work in canter. With a fairly large ride, canter can be introduced in a number of ways. All of the following options might be used with riders who can already manage the horse reasonably capably in and out of canter. (These would not be suitable exercises for riders experiencing their first or early canter lessons.)

Option (g) – Each rider leaves the ride to canter a circle individually.

Keep the whole ride on a circle at one end (because this class has eight riders, then probably keep them in walk; with fewer riders you may keep the ride in trot). Decrease the circle (let's assume it's at A) to 18m (this puts the ride just off the track, leaving room for one rider to pass on the outside). One rider leaves the 18m circle to the outside of the ride and takes trot. They change the rein over X and ride on a circle at the other end (at C). Once on their new circle on their own, they establish canter in their own time and canter one (20m) circle, returning to trot at the same place that they first took canter, they then change the rein again over X and return to the main ride, taking walk again and slotting into a space in the ride. Each rider repeats the individual canter exercise.

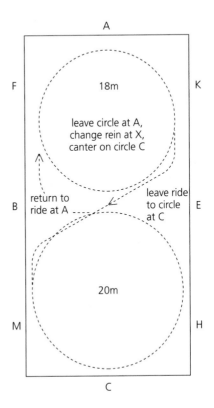

A

F   K
           18m

        leave circle at A,
        change rein at X,
        canter on circle C

        return to   leave ride
B   ride at A   to circle   E
                                     at C

             20m

M   H

C

Look out for any of the following:

- Rider losing control and effect when asked to ride away from the ride to the other end. (Improve the rider's resolve, preparation, aid application and effect.)

- Rider unable to establish canter through lack of effect. (Same remedy as above.)

- Rider unable to sustain the canter for a whole circle. (Same remedy as above.)

- Rider unable to execute a good-shaped circle in canter. (Same remedy as above.)

- Horse dictating the transition, especially falling back to trot. (Same remedy as above.)

Option (h) – Four riders cantering on a circle, as a ride.

As earlier in the lesson, divide the ride into four riders on one rein circling at A, and the other four on a circle in the opposite direction at C. Work one group of riders at a time; the other group can walk on their circle, staying in open order and watching the work.

Suggested command might be:

'First ride, space out well and all prepare to canter. Then canter.'

Each rider must take responsibility for staying in a space on the circle; if necessary, riders must steady or circle away to avoid getting too close to another rider. Repeat with the second group while the first group rest.

This exercise is challenging but teaches riders to concentrate and keep their horse balanced and controlled. You need to be sure that the horses are sensible enough to stay rhythmical and not become too 'sharp'.

- Watch for riders becoming tense and applying the aids a little abruptly rather than risk losing control.

- Encourage riders to find their balance and sense of rhythm and to keep the circle large enough.

- Encourage riders not to lean forward and begin to use too much body movement.

- Tell them when to start thinking of circling away if their timing is not very good.

Often riders need a little time to adjust to reacting more quickly in the faster paces.

Option (i) – Leading file leaves the ride to canter a circle and rejoin the rear of the ride.

It may be an option to work the class in a closed ride and use a basic canter exercise individually.

Suggested command:

'The whole ride, form up a ride behind So-and-So as leading file. Work with half a horse's length between each horse, and try to maintain these distances. Leading file in succession go forward to trot and canter, and at the free end of the school, canter a circle of 20m and then go large to take the rear of the ride.'

Riders will need help in the following areas:

- Preparation from a good, active trot, then balancing the horse (usually in a corner) to encourage the horse to move comfortably and fluently into the next pace.

- Riders should be reminded of the aids. Often it is the persistent repetition of aids, in this case for canter, that eventually ensures that the rider can reproduce the theoretical knowledge and apply it practically.

- Riders need encouragement to help them ride an active downward transition and prevent the horse from just falling out of canter and back into a running, unbalanced trot.

- Riders need help to correct any positional faults.

- Riders need practice.

The work described in this plan could potentially last at least an hour with a class of riders who were keen to progress.

Lesson Plan 2
Six riders just off the lead rein

SIX RIDERS WHO ARE JUST OFF THE LEAD REIN (OR LUNGE). THEY ARE READY TO START WORK IN A GROUP LESSON AND HAVE RIDDEN IN-DEPENDENTLY ONLY A FEW TIMES, IN A SMALL GROUP, FOR HALF AN HOUR AT A TIME, AND ALWAYS WITH SOMEONE TO LEAD THEM, IF NECESSARY.

Let's assume your riders are mounted on school horses that are suitable for and used to carrying novice riders.

IT IS ADVISABLE TO HAVE A COMPETENT LEADING FILE TO HELP IN THIS TYPE OF LESSON. This could be a trainee instructor, who can learn from the instructor while he or she helps out as leading file; or it could be a more competent rider from a different group who enjoys taking on this role; or it could be a competent 'weekend helper' riding another school horse.

Before each and every lesson:

- The ride must be safely accompanied to the school with their horses/ponies.

- The riders should be assisted with their mounting, making sure that stirrups and girths are correctly adjusted and comfortable to the rider.

- The instructor should find out the names of each rider and ask whether they are comfortable and happy.

Your first aims should be:

- To decide what basic competence your riders have.

- To ensure that everyone is confident and clear on what they are to do.

- To find out who is nervous or worried at any stage of the lesson.

Once all the riders are safely and comfortably mounted:

- Take your leading file and organise the rest of the riders behind them.

'Taking So-and-So as leading file, I would like you to form up a ride in the following order: So-and-So, walk forward and take the left [or right] rein, and A follow, then B, then C ...'

and so on until the order is designated.

The first priority is to have the ride walking in single file on the outside track, with half a horse's distance between them. Teaching riders to maintain distances is an art in itself. The rider must learn to estimate the correct distance behind the horse in front. As a rule: if the rider can see the tip of the horse's tail in front of them, then they are approximately half a horse's length behind that horse; if they cannot see the end of the tail, they are too close; and if they can see its heels and some ground surface as well, then they are too far away.

Teaching riders to maintain distances depends on teaching them to think ahead and not letting them get too close and/or making them ride more forward if they are getting left behind.

When the ride can maintain a good rhythm in the walk, maintaining good distances, then it is time to do some transitions.

'The whole ride prepare to halt ... and halt.'

Look for the riders preparing the movement by shortening their reins and making their position more secure. Ongoing correction of the rider's position would be appropriate throughout this lesson.

'The whole ride prepare to walk ... and walk on.'

When one or two transitions have been made, then a change of rein would be appropriate and the same work repeated on the other rein, before considering whether to move up into some trot work.

'It is time to work in trot. The whole ride, behind your leading file, prepare to trot (rising) ... and trot.'

It is important that the leading file sets a pace that the ride can keep up with – not too fast, but nevertheless forward enough for all the riders to settle into a rhythm in rising trot.

Several transitions could be made from walk to trot and from trot to walk. You would then be able to identify which riders managed the transitions quite well, and which were less co-ordinated or lacked thought or preparation.

You might consider the following exercise:

'Leading file, in succession, go forward to trot rising and go large to the rear of the ride.'

During this exercise look for the rider:

- Maintaining balance and correct position.

- Preparing for the transitions.

- Controlling the pace away from the ride and returning to the rear of the ride.

Novice riders usually benefit from some period of work without stirrups. This work helps to develop their depth of seat and independence and can be carried out as a ride in closed order or as part of an individual exercise.

Once you have halted your ride:

'Everyone quit and cross your stirrups over. Make sure that you pull the buckle away from the saddle so that it does not cause you discomfort. Cross the right stirrup over first and then the left, so that if you need to dismount you can drop the left stirrup over easily to remount. Once without stirrups, try to sit in the centre of the saddle and allow yourself to relax into the horse/pony.'

Make sure you correct all the riders' positions without stirrups, initially in halt and later in walk, as it is easy for the rider to adopt an incorrect position which, if not corrected from the outset, becomes established. The rider must feel confident about riding without stirrups and you must be on the look-out for variations in riders' confidence levels over this or any other activity on the horse.

Small periods of work in trot as a ride could ensue. Remember it is usually during the transitions that the balance and co-ordination of the rider are lost. Do not over-tire your novice riders: a small amount of work without stirrups is very beneficial, but too much can make them stiffer and then less keen to try again.

Line the ride up again to retake their stirrups.

Discuss with them what, if anything, they feel is different in their work without stirrups. It is important when teaching riders, that you encourage them from the earliest stage to be aware of 'what they can feel' with the horse's movement. This will develop their self-awareness, and therefore their control, more effectively.

You may then choose one of the following options for the latter part of the lesson.

Option (a) – Riding a 20m circle, first in walk, then in trot; first as a ride, then individually.

Option (b) – Rear file, in succession, halt and stay in halt until the ride comes around then rejoin as leading file.

Option (c) – Leading file, in succession, turn across the school from E or B, halt on the centre line and trot away to take the rear of the ride.

Option (a)

'As a ride behind your leading file, the whole ride prepare to trot ... and trot. The ride circle at A or C, 20m .... The whole ride, prepare to walk ... and walk. Then leading file, in succession, forward to trot, go large and leave the ride. Circle 20m at the free end of the school, then go large and join the rear of the ride.'

The whole ride follows the leading file on a 20m circle at A or C. It can also be ridden at B or E, but initially it is easier to ride it at A or C where the walls of the

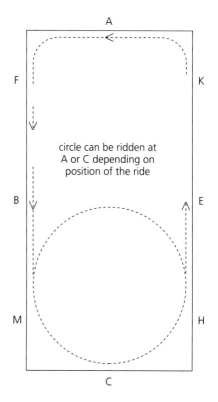

circle can be ridden at A or C depending on position of the ride

school, or boards of an outside school, make it easier to visualise the shape and size. If your riders have never ridden a 20m circle it may be helpful to draw the pattern or shape in the sand in front of them. Alternatively (and this is usually very successful), walk the figure yourself and encourage them to follow you so that they learn the floor pattern. When the ride can follow each other on the circle with some understanding of the aids, which are:

– inside leg on the girth to maintain the forwardness and the bend;

– outside leg, slightly behind the girth, to hold the hindquarters and prevent them from slipping out;

– inside rein maintaining a slight flexion in the direction of the movement;

– outside rein controlling the degree of bend in the neck and also regulating the pace;

then you may ask each rider to trot to the rear of the ride on the circle.

■ Assist in preparation and execution of the trot.

■ Assist in guiding the shape of the circle (stand at X ,or put cones around the circle to help the rider gauge the shape of the figure).

■ Be aware of any horses/ponies who may take advantage of the novice rider, making some decisions about the speed of the pace. Many school horses can be encouraged to react to your voice, so if you urge the horse to go forward you help the rider to achieve a better balance and circle shape. Also, the horse produces better quality work, therefore giving the rider a better understanding of the quality of the gaits.

Option (b)

'Rear file, in succession, make a transition to halt [walk first if the ride are in trot], stand still until the ride comes around behind you, and then, through a few steps of walk, move into trot and take the lead.'

This exercise asserts the rider's authority and can be quite challenging for the novice rider. The horse may be reluctant to stop when his 'friends' are moving away from him. Similarly, he may want to jog to follow the group when he should stand still and wait. Furthermore, he may not be keen to move back into trot once his 'friends' are behind him. Again, this is an exercise where an instructor with careful, tactful authority in his or her voice can influence the horse to fulfil the requirements of the movement to assist the rider.

The following should be emphasised:

- The rider's need to prepare and think ahead and apply the aids with firmness and conviction.

- The rider's need to look ahead for where to make the transitions.

- The need to maintain balance and position.

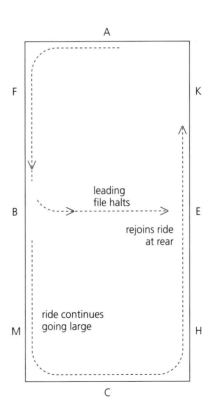

Option (c)

'Leading file, turn across at E or B and then halt at X, wait, then proceed in trot and turn to take the rear of the ride as the ride comes around.'

This exercise requires:

- Thinking ahead from the rider, to gauge when to turn at E or B. You, the instructor, can assist in advising when to turn.

- Keeping the horse straight and preparing for the halt at X.

- Keeping the horse quietly standing in halt until time to move off.

- Riding forward straight, into a good turn at the opposite wall, and not allowing the horse to fall in on returning to the track.

- Guidance from you as to when the rider should start to give the aids for the transitions.

Most lessons, particularly those involving fairly novice or inexperienced riders, benefit from spending the first few minutes and the last few minutes working with the ride as a whole. Whether that work is in walk or in trot, or a little of both, will depend on the confidence of your riders, and later, towards the end of the lesson, on how physically tired they might be. If the lesson has been quite challenging and the riders are looking a little weary, then spending the last few minutes in walk may be a welcome relief. It also gives you the chance to recap on any work you feel you want to leave fresh in the riders' minds, or allow for any questions to be asked.

Lesson Plan 3
Six riders starting to work on jumping

SIX RIDERS WHO HAVE BEEN RIDING FOR SOME TIME ON A WEEKLY BASIS. THEY RIDE ONE HOUR PER WEEK WITH THE OCCASIONAL EXTRA ESCORTED HACK OUT. THEY ALL FEEL CONFIDENT IN WALK, TROT AND CANTER, WITH AND WITHOUT STIRRUPS, AND HAVE DONE A SMALL AMOUNT OF JUMPING. YOU HAVE TAUGHT THESE RIDERS BEFORE.

- All the riders are mounted on school horses which they have ridden before on more than one occasion.

- All the riders have mounted safely and are comfortable with their stirrups and have checked their girths.

Your first aim should be to:

- Reacquaint yourself with each rider, find out how they are feeling 'today'.

- Be aware if a rider is feeling 'not very confident', or is 'tired' after a busy week at work or school.

- Perhaps ask what everyone would like to do in the lesson to give you some idea of your rider's expectations.

- Give some broad ideas about the possible extent of the work you hope to cover, e.g. 'Today we will practice some transitions between the paces, then work on making the jumping position more secure, aiming towards some jumping later in the lesson.'

To work the ride in, you could choose:

Option (a) – to work them in open order.

or

Option (b) – to work them in closed order as a ride.

Taking **option (b)**:

'The whole ride, with So-and-So as leading file and in the following order [describe the order], prepare to walk out onto the left/right rein and go large in walk. The whole ride walk march.'

'Keeping the distances at half a horse's length, the whole ride prepare to trot rising, and the ride trot.'

Work the ride in trot for a minute or two concentrating on:

- Correct rider position

 – straight line from ear, to shoulder, to hip to heel.

 – with a second straight line from elbow to wrist, to horse's mouth.

- Maintaining a rhythm and forwardness in the trot.

- The riders' ability to ride fairly good corners with the horse bending a little through each corner. The horse must be looking in the direction of the movement.

'The whole ride change the rein from – to – across the long diagonal.'

During the change of rein help the riders to:

- Be aware of maintaining the forwardness of the trot and then hopefully keep the rhythm secure.

- Be aware of smoothly changing the bend into the new direction.

- Encourage the diagonal to be changed at the end of the diagonal line and not half way across the middle at X; the latter may interfere with the rhythm and show particularly at a later stage, when medium trot is introduced.

- Encourage the rhythm, impulsion and bend (including the change of bend) to stay the same, and when all these criteria are consistent (into the new rein), then change over the whip (if carried). The whip change is the least important part of a change of rein and it must not disturb the other, much more valuable criteria.

Work similarly on the new rein for a short time until the riders are secure and consistent in the trot rhythm.

'**The whole ride prepare to walk ... and the ride walk. Make much of your horses and let them have a longer rein to stretch for a minute or two.**'

'**The next exercise will be ridden individually from front to rear of the ride. Leading file, in succession, go forward to trot. In the first corner you come to, take sitting trot and ask for canter. Canter to the free end of the school and ride a 20m circle, then go large to take the rear of the ride in trot, and then walk.**' (This is similar in pattern to the exercise shown on page 106.)

As the leading file commences, watch for:

- The rider preparing the horse by making sure that the trot is forward enough and the aids for canter are clearly applied in a corner.

- The rider being sufficiently effective to ride the horse away from the ride when he might be reluctant to leave the other horses.

- The rider preparing adequately, so that the horse does not fall out of canter when he chooses to slow down of his own accord.

- The rider maintaining a good position throughout the exercise without leaning forward or using excessive body movement.

- The rider allowing the canter to happen without restriction through the hands or arms.

- Guidance may be needed to advise the rider of where to ride the circle to keep furthest away from the ride.

- Preparation will be needed for a good downward transition.

You may decide to repeat this exercise on the other rein. And/or your riders could do this exercise without their stirrups, which would help deepen their positions and increase their independence.

Depending on what period of time you wish to allocate for jumping, you may start the jump work at this stage of the lesson, or you may work a little longer on the flat and then start jumping.

Let us assume that you are now going to start the jumping part of the lesson.

Find out from your riders:

- Whether they are all keen to jump. (Hopefully you will not have any riders who do not wish to jump, but if you do, remember this for next time and try to organise things so that class members have similar ambitions.)

- Whether they have jumped before.

- How confident they feel about jumping.

If you have taught this ride before you will know how much the riders understand about the 'jumping position'. If in doubt, or if you think there may be some riders who have forgotten the information about jumping position, then you should recap on it. Teaching jumping position, as with the basic position on the flat, is an ongoing task for the riding teacher. Every rider should always be looking to improve his balance and security, whether on the flat or over jumps.

When discussing the jumping position, perhaps use one rider to demonstrate it (at halt).

When teaching jumping position it is important that:

- The rider's stirrups are one to two holes shorter than usual, so that the security of the position is enhanced. Always look at the physique of the rider before correcting position – it may be that the rider has very short arms or a heavy seat. Any corrections made should be with the best interests of the horse at heart.

- The rider's position should be in balance, with the reins short enough, and the rider's lower leg well in support of the upper body.

- The weight, balance and security are all dependent on the rider developing a secure but independent position which is able to 'follow' the horse in the air over fences.

- This security of the lower leg is the basis for developing the balance, effect and feel of the rider.

Demonstrate the jumping position in a group situation if possible, so that everyone can learn from each other. Once each rider has been encouraged to adopt the jumping position in halt, then move on into trot and in due course into canter, working to ensure that each rider has the balance and co-ordination to maintain good control.

'As a ride, behind So-and-So, your leading file, the whole ride walk march onto the left rein and encourage the horses to go forward in a good rhythm. Maintain the distances at half a horse's length. In succession, take trot and canter to the rear of the ride. On the long sides of the school, take jumping position, and on the short side maintain the body position but allow the horse to shorten the trot a little (with rounder, higher steps) to find balance around the corners.'

Jumping position can then be practised in trot or canter depending on the rider's balance and confidence. Individually riders can then be encouraged to trot or canter to the rear of the ride while demonstrating the development of the jumping position.

Starting to jump

There are various places where jumping equipment can be safely positioned in the school without interfering with the lesson in progress. Stored equipment poses a potential problem when horses are moving in and around it; this needs to be considered against the impracticality of having to move equipment from outside the school into the arena every time you give a jumping lesson.

Start with one pole on the three-quarter line positioned around E or B. In this position the riders will have to ride a good corner and line of approach to the centre of the pole, and ride away in a straight departure to another good corner back onto the track. (See diagram overleaf.)

The ride should be spaced so that there are at least two horses' lengths between each rider; or the ride could work in open order. Both situations need control and awareness from the instructor. In open order riders must be clear about how to circle away without interfering with the approach to or departure from the pole. If working in ride order each rider must be capable of controlling his or her horse so that it does not hurry and get too close to the horse in front of it. Working in ride order is only practical in work over a single pole; if several poles are used the riders must be spaced further apart, so that if poles are knocked out of place they can be readjusted before the next rider approaches.

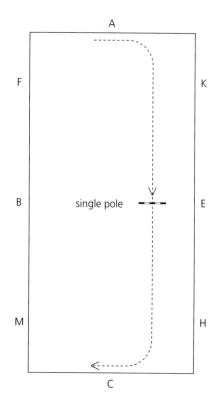

On the three-quarter line riders may approach from either direction (left or right rein).

During this preparation for jumping look for:

■ Riders being able to maintain the rhythm and energy on a straight line to the pole.

■ Riders being able to adopt a balanced jumping position in the approach to and over the pole.

■ Riders being able to maintain the same tempo (speed) in the trot in the approach and departure.

■ Riders executing a good corner and a straight line to the pole.

Once one pole has been negotiated then three poles could be used, spaced at approximately 4ft 6ins (1.3m) apart (see diagram opposite, left). Three is prefer-

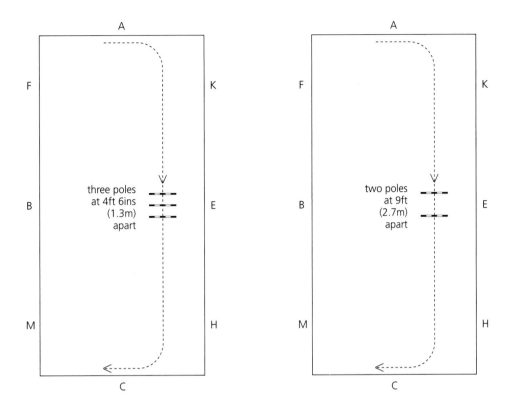

able to two, which can present an optical illusion to the horse and cause him to jump them. If choosing to use two poles, they must be double-spaced (at 9ft/2.7m) so that it is clear to the horse that he should step between them (see diagram above right).

Riders should then be encouraged to come to the poles either in groups of three or four (working in open order while the other three/four riders rest and watch), then the groups swap over. Riders should come two or three times to the poles so that they can practise establishing a good rhythm and position over them.

When the trotting pole work is secure then a small jump can be introduced. Either the three trotting poles can be maintained and a small fence added, or one pole can be used as a 'placing pole' in front of a small fence (see diagram overleaf). Both of these methods will generate the same result, which should be that the rider can approach the pole(s) in trot and then smoothly jump the small fence while maintaining balance and position.

115

Riders should be encouraged to repeat the jump several times until they can achieve at least two efforts which are evenly matched and consistent in result.

While jumping, the instructor wants to see:

- A good corner and line of approach.

- The ability to maintain energy in the trot in the approach.

- The ability to control the approach and not allow the horse to quicken and dictate the speed.

- The ability to keep a balanced position in the air. If this is difficult then encourage the rider to hold the horse's mane to help improve their balance, security and feel.

- The ability to control the departure with regard to speed, line and rider's balance.

A

F   K

placing pole
9ft (2.7m) in
front of fence

B   E

M   H

C

The work described would easily occupy a class ride for an hour. It should be remembered that while having a plan in your mind, circumstances may prevent you from progressing as you had intended – you must always teach what is happening in front of you. Sometimes this will mean that you are unable to progress as much as you had hoped, or, on other occasions when all the riders are working very competently, you may find that you progress through work much more quickly. It is helpful always to have one or two extra options that you could use to fill any time left at the end of a lesson.

If the ride has worked hard and the horses deserve a little breather, choose something at the end of a lesson which will still tax your riders and not let them feel that they have been short-changed on their lesson. The following examples may give you one or two ideas.

- Return to an exercise with the ride in closed order. **'Leading file, in succession, go forward to trot and by E or B walk for FOUR STRIDES then trot again to the rear of the ride.'** This exercise confirms that riders understand the difference between **STRIDES** and **STEPS** and also makes them aware of how essential 'preparation' is . This exercise is almost impossible to do well without good preparation.

- **'In open order, the ride walk around the school in medium walk. On each long side allow your horse to take the rein forward into a free walk on a long rein.'** This exercise teaches the rider about the difference between medium walk and free walk on a long rein.

- **'Leading file, in succession, go forward to trot and turn onto the centre line. At X make a transition to halt and then move off in trot, making a good turn at the other end of the centre line.'** This exercise teaches riders to use the centre line accurately and prepares them for eventually being able to ride a dressage test.

Lesson Plan 4
Six child riders ready to start cantering

SIX CHILD RIDERS WHO HAVE BEEN RIDING FOR A FEW MONTHS. THEY HAVE WALKED AND TROTTED, WITH AND WITHOUT THEIR STIRRUPS, AND MOST OF THEM ARE READY TO START CANTERING. FOR SOME IT WILL BE THEIR FIRST CANTER LESSON; FOR THE OTHERS THEY WILL ONLY HAVE CANTERED ONCE OR TWICE. YOU HAVE NEVER TAUGHT THESE RIDERS BEFORE, BUT THEY ARE MOUNTED ON SCHOOL PONIES/HORSES THAT ARE FAMILIAR TO YOU.

- All the riders are mounted and have had their stirrups and girths adjusted and checked.

- All the riders have ridden the horse/pony they are mounted on at least once before.

Your first aim is:

- Make sure you know all the riders' names. Ask one or two questions of each rider so that they 'know' you and feel that you are interested in them. Perhaps ask them what they want to do today?

- Make sure that the early work allows you to see the strengths and weaknesses of the riders and how they are riding today, on the animal on which they are mounted.

- If you know the horses/ponies then work them in an order that is likely to produce the best results.

- If your aim is ultimately canter then you should work towards security, control and effect, and the following might be appropriate:

'With So-and-So as leading file, the whole ride walk forward to the track in the following order [describe the order], and go large on the right/left rein.'

'Whole ride prepare to trot rising ... and the ride trot. Maintain the distances at half a horse's length.'

During this initial working in:

- Observe and make corrections to each rider's position.

- Observe control of distances and influence over the horse.

- Observe overall balance and co-ordination of each rider.

The next exercise will give you some idea of how much control and determination each rider has.

'With the ride working in trot, from the rear of the ride, rear file come forward to walk and then to halt. Stay in halt for a few seconds and then go forward to walk. Stay in walk until the ride comes around behind you and then trot as leading file.'

It is hoped that each rider carries out this exercise on an obedient school horse and is in control and able to influence the basic transitions.

'The ride, make a 20m circle at A or C. Stay on this circle, and the whole ride prepare to walk ... the ride, walk.'

Then halt the ride and ask them to quit and cross their stirrup irons (stirrups should be out of the way of the rider's leg and lie across the horse's wither immediately in front of the saddle). Ask the ride to proceed in walk and stay on the circle. Then ask them to take trot. Walk and trot as a ride for short periods paying particular attention to the riders' position and balance.

In the work without stirrups:

- The riders should stay relaxed and learn to absorb the movement of the horse through the small of the back; they should avoid gripping up with their legs.

- The riders should try to keep their hands steady and not use the reins to maintain their balance and position. If necessary, they should hold the front of the saddle if they feel their balance is at risk.

- The riders must be able to maintain control of the trot, keeping the pace going and controlling the speed.

- The riders must be able to move smoothly from walk to trot, and from trot to walk.

All the above criteria should be fairly well established before it would be wise to introduce canter. Additionally, **THE RIDER MUST WANT TO LEARN TO CANTER.**

After the work without stirrups allow the riders to take their stirrups back and feel settled and more secure in the saddle. Hopefully all the riders will have seen canter before (if in the unlikely case that one has not, then you may need to demonstrate the canter using one of your pupil's horses).

For novice riders, too much explanation about a new activity can be confusing and overloading. They need basic information which will enable them to achieve the aim and enough awareness of how to develop the skill.

Information prior to the first canter lesson:

- Canter is the next pace up from trot. It is a little faster than trot, and, unlike the trot where we have learned to rise or sit, in canter we aim to sit in the saddle and absorb the movement through our back and seat.

- We ask for canter in a corner because that is where it is easiest for the horse to take canter.

- You will aim to increase the energy of the trot a little as you approach the first corner, then as you go into the second corner try to cease rising trot and give a little kick with both legs, and hold the neck strap for added security. The horse/pony should then take canter.

- When you feel the canter, try to sit up and slide your seat from the back to the front (rather like the movement of sitting on a swing and trying to make it go higher without your legs touching the ground).

- Try to keep you shoulders back over your hips and just allow your hips to swing.

- At the end of the long side, try to stay tall in your position and ease back with both reins, which will ask the horse to slow down. When you feel the horse come down to trot, try to establish rising trot, because the trot will be fairly active and you will find it quite hard to take sitting trot in the early stages.

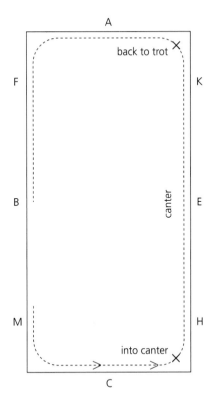

It is then your responsibility, as the instructor, to make sure that the first canter lesson actually happens as you have described it. This is where the use of well-trained school horses is so important. In conjunction with your positioning near the corner and knowledge of the horse's reaction to your voice, you should be able to 'talk' the novice rider through the first canter so that the horse does exactly what you have described. In the case of small children riding ponies it is even possible to run alongside (depending on how fit you are!) and help the rider into canter and back to trot again.

If a pupil is keen to learn canter then the first canter should be exciting and hugely satisfying for the rider; it should be something he is anxious to repeat, and repetition is the key to competence.

Always aim for the riders cantering from the second corner (of a short side) down just one long side of the school for the first few times until they are confident in the feeling of the canter, then gradually introduce longer periods of canter incorporating a short side and then eventually going around the whole school. Work on both reins and keep a very careful eye on the confidence of each rider. If a rider is reluctant to canter then do not pressurise him, often he may need to watch others to motivate him into 'having a go'. Sometimes the rider may need to be mounted on another horse/pony who moves more easily into canter. It should never become an issue if one rider in a group does not

121

achieve the same standard as the others, as long as the confidence of that rider is maintained and they feel valued and competent at their level.

The canter should be practised on both reins.

After some work towards developing canter the class might return to trot exercises and could work as follows:

- **'We will return to work in single file behind the leading file; keep distances at half a horse's length.'**

- **'Whole ride, in single file, from A or C, ride a three-loop serpentine, each loop going to the outside of the arena.'**

- **'Aim to ride three loops of equal size and shape and practise changing the bend through each change of direction.'**

- **'If you understand about diagonals in trot then try to change your diagonal every time you change the direction over the centre line.'**

- **'Feel the same rhythm in the trot throughout the exercise.'**

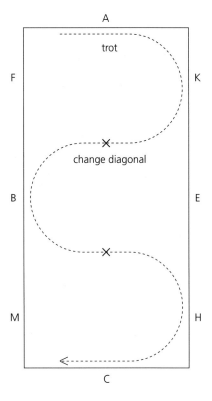

This exercise could also be ridden individually, with the ride staying in walk while leading file, in succession, goes forward to trot and rides a three-loop serpentine from A or C (whichever comes first), and then goes large to take the rear of the ride.

The first canter is a big milestone in most rider's lives and so the lesson where the rider achieves this is quite special. Be aware of this and add much praise and encouragement to what is a big achievement in the mind of the fairly new rider. Try to ensure that the rider goes away with a very positive feeling about learning to canter.

Lesson Plan 5
Six competent riders learning to improve basic lateral work

SIX RIDERS WHO HAVE BEEN RIDING FOR SEVERAL YEARS. THEY ARE ADOLESCENTS AND YOUNG ADULTS. ALTHOUGH RIDING ONLY ONCE A WEEK, THEY ARE ALL COMPETENT IN WALK, TROT AND CANTER AND HAVE WORKED WITHOUT THEIR STIRRUPS IN ALL THREE PACES ON NUMEROUS OCCASIONS. THEY HAVE A BASIC UNDERSTANDING OF TURNS ON THE FOREHAND AND LEG YIELD.

- The ride is mounted on school horses that they have ridden frequently; and you regularly teach this ride.

- The ride are mounted and their stirrups and girths are comfortable and secure.

'We will work in in open order. In your own time go forward to the track and start on the right rein. Work in open order in walk and trot, do not change the rein until I say. If you get too close to other riders then circle away to maintain a space between you and other horses.'

Aim:

- For forward, rhythmical paces and the rider sitting in as good a balance and position as possible.

- For concentration and relaxation, with the rider beginning to focus on the lesson and work for improvement.

'The whole ride in your own time, make a change of rein.'

Look for:

- How the riders choose to change the rein. It should be thought out and ridden with care; they should not just throw the horse across the first line they can think of.

- The riders clearly maintaining the rhythm and forwardness and changing the bend of the horse before taking the new direction.

- The riders prioritising rhythm, forwardness, smooth change of bend, and fluency throughout. If the whip can also be changed simultaneously without losing any of the above criteria, then this is good but not essential; the whip can be changed once the rider has taken the new rein.

'Continue working on the other rein, aiming to achieve a rhythmical, relaxed and forward-going trot.'

'Within the work in trot include some 20m circles at either A or C, whenever the end is free.'

'It is now time to introduce transitions into the work to help improve your horse's response to the aids and to make him more supple and so easier to ride. The transition can be made across the centre line, by making a turn off the track, riding the transition over the centre and then retaking trot on the next long side. The transition can be through walk and/or also into halt, and then away in walk or trot.' (See diagram on page 96.)

Throughout the transition work you, the instructor, should be looking for:

- The rider's ability to follow the horse's movement and stay in balance through a variety of paces and transitions.

- The rider's preparation for the transition.

- The rider's ability to execute the transition with co-ordination and harmony with the horse.

'We will now move on into canter work and incorporate some turns on the forehand.'

Turn on the forehand is a useful exercise to:

- Improve the horse's suppleness and response to the rider's aids.

- Improve the rider's co-ordination and feel for the horse moving under him.

'We will work as a ride in closed order for the next exercise. With So-and-So as leading file, form a ride in the following order: A, then B, then C and so on.'

'The ride on the left rein, in walk. Leading file, in succession, go forward to trot, make a change of rein across the first long diagonal, go large to the A or C marker, forward to halt, make a left turn on the forehand and then forward to trot and canter to take the rear of the ride.'

The aids for the turn on the forehand are:

- Inside rein creates a hint of flexion in the neck.

- Inside leg (on the girth, or, if necessary, a little behind) asks the hindquarters to move over.

- Outside rein controls the pace (prevents the horse from moving forward) and regulates the degree of bend in the neck.

- Outside leg behind the girth controls the hindquarters and prevents them from swinging out.

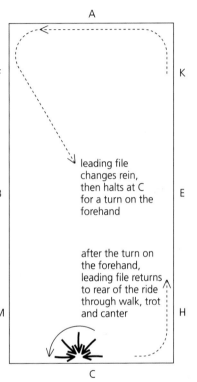

leading file changes rein, then halts at C for a turn on the forehand

after the turn on the forehand, leading file returns to rear of the ride through walk, trot and canter

The horse steps around the forelegs by moving the inside hind leg over and in front of the outside hind leg. 'Inside' and 'outside' always refer to the direction in which the horse is bent. In this case if the turn on the forehand is to the left, then the bend is to the left, and the inside leg and hand are the left hand and leg, and the outside hand and leg are the right hand and leg. The horse completes a 180° turn.

Within this exercise look for:

- The trot not going forward enough into the change of rein.

- Lack of preparation for the halt.

- Halt not balanced so the horse not able to respond well to the aids for turn on the forehand.

- Lack of feel for the steps in the turn on the forehand.

- The horse rushing the steps.

- The rider allowing the horse to move forward out of the movement.

- The rider restricting the horse and causing it to step backwards from the halt.

- Poor preparation for the canter transition.

- The rider losing position and leaning in or gripping up with the legs in the turn on the forehand.

This exercise actually prepares the horse very well for the canter transition, which can be made easily from walk (or trot) because the turn on the forehand has put the horse more 'on the aids'. It could be repeated on the other rein so that the riders have cantered on both reins.

Alternatively another canter exercise could be used as follows:

'Leading file in succession go forward to trot, in the first corner you come to when the horse is balanced, go forward to canter. Half way along the next long side make a half 20m circle across the school and then go large to take the rear of the ride. The rest of the ride remain in trot ... leading file commence.'

In this exercise look for:

- The rider preparing the canter transition well.

- The rider applying the aids for canter while maintaining a good basic position.

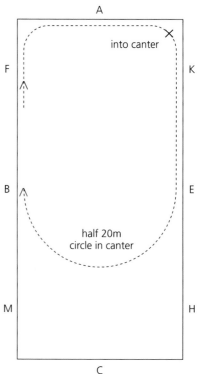

126

- The rider keeping the same rhythm and speed of canter around the school and into the half circle.

- The rider preparing the downward transition to enable the horse to make a balanced transition back to trot.

If this group is working well in all three paces – walk, trot and canter – then any of the work described above could be done with the riders without stirrups. Remember that a person who rides only once each week cannot be as 'riding fit' as a someone who rides every day or rides several horses two or three times a week. It is important that you use judgement in working riders without their stirrups. The work must ultimately improve their depth, suppleness, balance and effectiveness. It must not make them so uncomfortable that any benefit is negated by the resulting aching muscles!

You may now choose to introduce some leg yielding into the work. Leg yield can be used successfully in many different ways in the school and to benefit both horses and riders. With any ride, but certainly with weekly riders, always recap as follows:

- Leg yield is a movement where the horse is asked to move forwards and sideways away from the direction in which he is flexed.

- In leg yield the horse is almost straight, with just a hint of direction through the 'gullet'; the inside hind leg steps forward and across under the horse's centre of gravity, slightly in front of and crossing towards the outside hind leg.

- In leg yield the horse **MUST** maintain the forward movement and must never end up going more sideways than he does forwards.

- The sideways movement is in addition to the forward movement, never instead of it.

Leg yield is a useful exercise when executed correctly, but there is a possibility that the horse may learn to evade 'working' whilst performing it, and drop behind the rider or cross sideways more than stay forwards.

Leg yield can be ridden anywhere in the school but here we will describe it as if from the three-quarter line back to the wall.

The aids for leg yield are:

- First to have the horse straight.

- The inside rein maintains a degree of flexion.

- The inside leg on the girth (or a little behind it, without pushing the hindquarters out) asks the horse to go more forward into the outside rein.

- The outside rein does not allow the horse to go more forward and so the extra energy takes the inside inside hind leg forward and across under the body in the leg-yield steps.

Start with the ride in open order and have them riding good turns along the three-quarter line. Once the rider can learn to ride along that line maintaining straightness and ride a good turn again back onto the track through a good corner also, then he is ready to leg yield.

You might prompt your riders as follows:

'Turn onto the three-quarter line in walk or trot. When the horse is straight, increase the pressure of your inside leg and maintain the contact and control of the pace. The horse should then move forwards and sideways back to the track. The horse's body should remain straight and parallel to the outside wall. As he responds to the inside leg, he should remain straight and not fall out through the outside shoulder.'

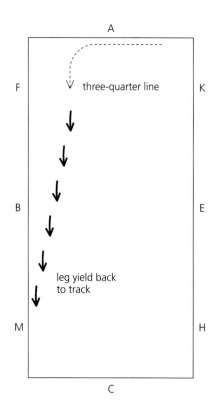

In using this exercise look for the following:

- Poor corners and turns onto the three-quarter line.

- The horse not straight on the line, either falling out through the outside shoulder or falling in. In both cases it is the rider's balance and co-ordination which inhibit the horse from staying straight.

- Too much inside neck bend and leg, which encourages the horse to fall out through the shoulder and hurry away from the inside leg.

- The rider losing his central position in the saddle and leaning inwards or outwards as he asks the horse to move sideways.

- The rider's inside hand crossing over the line of the neck to the outside. The outside hand losing contact.

- The rider unaware of the importance of using his outside leg to support and balance the horse.

- The horse falling sideways at the expense of the forward movement.

- The horse slowing down or becoming resistant to the rider.

In all cases first look to the preparation, then improve the knowledge and co-ordination of the aids. Then improve through repetition. Ask your riders what they are feeling. Develop their awareness of the faults that you can identify but of which they may not be so conscious.

Leg yield can be used in walk or trot and is easily used in open order. Riders may then take their own lines and corners and choose their pace to best advantage. You should position yourself at the end of the three-quarter line with the rider coming towards you. It is then easy to monitor the riding of the corner, the straightness prior to asking for the leg yield, the leg yield itself and the corner at the end of the line. From this position it is also easy to see whether the rider's legs are equally on the horse, how straight the rider is and how much the horse's inside hind leg steps under the horse's body.

After some work on leg yield, finish the lesson with some basic trot work on circles or going large, and try to encourage the riders to feel a difference in the trot. Hopefully the trot should be:

- More secure in the rhythm.

- More forward to a steady rein content.

- More responsive to the basic aid application.

- More supple on both reins.

This work would keep a group of competent riders busy for at least an hour's class lesson, depending on what other eventualities the lesson threw up unexpectedly.

Lesson Plan 6
Six to eight riders improving their jumping

SIX TO EIGHT RIDERS WHO RIDE ON AVERAGE ONCE A WEEK IN THE RIDING SCHOOL. THEY ALL ENJOY JUMPING, AND THIS LESSON WILL BE A CLASS JUMPING LESSON. YOU HAVE TAUGHT THEM BEFORE AND THEY ARE ALL MOUNTED ON SCHOOL HORSES THEY HAVE RIDDEN BEFORE AND THAT YOU KNOW WELL.

The aim of the lesson will be to progress the ability and enjoyment of jumping within the group, by working towards jumping several fences linked together.

- The ride are all safely mounted and their stirrups and girths have been checked. They are all 'at jumping length'.

First the ride must be assessed on how they are riding today, and horses and riders must be 'worked in'.

This group should be familiar with working in open order.

'The whole ride, go large in open order on the left rein. Find a space and begin to work your horse in, using walk, trot and canter in your own time. Be aware of other riders, and if you meet someone on the opposite rein then pass left to left. Use transitions from one pace to another to begin to encourage your horse to be supple and obedient.'

While the working in is taking place you can begin to organise your jumps as long as you continue to observe your riders carefully and help them as necessary.

During the working in you would be looking for:

- The rider using good judgement about staying in a space, away from other riders and beginning to ride independently.

- The rider able to ride his horse forward with good rhythm in all paces, showing a confidence in control through the transitions.

- The rider demonstrating the ability to think ahead, with awareness of what other riders are doing and where they might be riding to.

- The rider maintaining good control through all three paces.

Specific working in towards jumping may be done as follows, but first halt the ride and make sure everyone is happy with their stirrups.

'**All check your girths now you have worked in for a while. The whole ride, now work as a ride in closed order behind So-and-So as leading file. The whole ride, walk march onto the track and take the right rein. In walk, the whole ride, on each long side take jumping position.'**

Make individual corrections of position as this is done. Then continue:

'**The whole ride, forward to trot, and then leading file, in succession, go forward to canter and go large to the rear of the ride. On each long side during this exercise take jumping position and on the short sides come upright again. Practise the feel of maintaining your balance in jumping position and in upright position.'**

A development of this exercise would be to send the canter on along the long side and 'shorten' the canter on the short sides. This exercise asks a little more of the rider in terms of balance and effort.

The rider's balance and security in jumping position is the critical issue here, because the rider's ultimate ability to stay with the horse throughout the jump is dependent on these factors. This area of teaching cannot be underestimated and the security of the jumping position must be worked on and consolidated in every jumping lesson.

Before jumping, walk the ride again and ask everyone to re-check their girth.

As the group have jumped before with you teaching them, you can progress to a jump initially unless:

- Any rider is showing signs of anxiety about jumping and asks for a pole on the ground to start.

- Any horse is proving to be lazy or a little stiff and a pole on the ground may motivate or loosen him prior to a jump.

- You have any doubts whatsoever about the competence or confidence of your group 'today'.

Position the first jump on the three-quarter line (in off the track), fairly central to E or B. The line of approach would therefore be along the three-quarter line, and the line of departure likewise. The jump may or may not have a placing pole in front of it. Usually the approach would be in trot but it could also be ridden in canter.

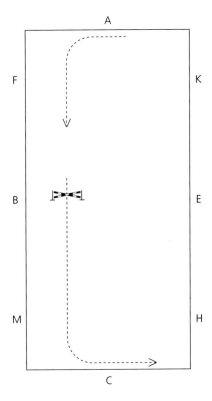

Depending on how competent your ride are, you can either have the whole ride working at the same time or you can split them into two groups (with three or four per group). One group rides and one group watches. With the group watching (stand them on the centre line) try to encourage them to watch 'actively', i.e. to be interested in the way the other ride performs because it may help them to deal with any problems when their time comes.

This fence could be jumped from both directions as required, from each rein in turn. Usually the first jump is built as a cross-pole (easier to keep the approach central by focusing on the middle of the fence).

Look for the following:

- Poor line of approach from a badly ridden corner.

- Horse either slowing down in the approach or speeding up.

- Loss of balance in the air.

- Dependence on the reins to maintain balance on the horse.

- Loss of position at any stage of the approach, jump or departure.

After everyone has jumped the first fence out of trot or canter (or perhaps first in trot with the placing pole and then in canter without the placing pole) then it is time to introduce a second fence. This jump could be put on the other side of the school, again on the three-quarter line. It may be another cross-pole or a small vertical fence (straight rail).

Now that you have introduced a second fence each rider should come individually to the jumps. The aim will be to ride the first fence (in trot or canter approach) then land in canter and keep a fluent canter around the top of the school and approach the second fence from canter. With six or eight riders in the school there are various ways you can 'manage' the ride safely.

Option (a) – All riders stay on the centre line while one rider carries out the exercise.

Advantages:
– Very safe, as only the rider jumping is on the move.
– You have only one rider to concentrate on.

Disadvantages:
– Horses and riders 'switch off' when standing still for a while and then may perform poorly when it is their time.

– The horse performing may be drawn back (napping) to his friends and therefore be reluctant to stay on line to the jump.

Option (b) – Four riders line up on the centre line. The other four riders go large around the school and one of those four comes to the jumps individually. Each rider from this group takes his turn.

Advantages:
– Four riders keep moving and have to concentrate on each other as well as their own horse.
– Horses are less likely to 'switch off'.
– Horses keep moving more, therefore the time taken to involve each rider is shorter so more can be done in the time allowed.

Disadvantages:
– You have got to be very aware and ensure that you are **always** watching the approach and departure to the fence so that you can deal with the unexpected (e.g. a horse stopping in front of a fence).
– You need to insist that the riders take responsibility for not getting in each other's way and stay alert to who is going to jump when.

Option (c) – All the riders are kept moving and one or two riders are asked to jump the fences when clear.

Advantages:
– All the horses stay much more involved and the riders do not need to be 'woken up' after standing around.
– The horses are far less likely to nap or hurry to try to catch up with their 'friends'.
– This simulates what a rider may have to deal with if they go to a show on their own.
– It improves their reactions, their independence and their ability to 'cope' with any eventuality.
– It develops them as riders far more than a lesson where the instructor takes most of the initiative about what is covered within that lesson.

Disadvantages:

– There is greater risk of an incident or collision because several horses are on the move at one time.

– A rider may inadvertently get in the way of another rider.

In riding from one jump to the other look for:

■ Good line of approach to the first fence.

■ Control of pace in approach and departure.

■ Maintenance of rider's position in approach, jump and departure.

■ Good line away from the first fence and a fluent rhythm from one fence to another, bearing in mind the straight line of approach to the second jump.

■ Maintenance of balance and rhythm away from the second fence.

When these two fences have been well negotiated then a change of rein could be involved between the first and second fence.

The jumps could then be repeated with the change of rein. The above criteria would apply again.

A third fence could then be introduced on the diagonal line. The riders would then be asked to ride from fence A, across the diagonal jumping fence B and then onto the new rein and jump fence C.

By this stage it is not practical any longer to 'park' some of the ride on the centre line. It is still possible, though, to have three riders moving carefully around the outside while the fourth rider jumps on the inside track; the other four riders would then halt in a corner each. Alternatively all other riders can stand in the corners, with just one rider

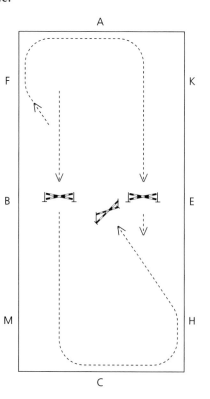

taking the whole school to jump the fences.

It is essential that you always know when a rider is going to make a line of approach to a jump. You may be talking to another rider, but your eyes must always be aware of who is jumping and how they are going about it.

Your small fences may be cross poles, small verticals or small ascending spread (oxer) fences.

The procedure described above would be one of the simplest ways of linking jumps together to encourage riders to think ahead and prepare for each fence.

Glossary

'Bend' The elastic, lateral suppleness in the horse's body from his hind legs through to his nose. The bend should be even through the horse's body and not only in the head and neck. On curved lines the horse's hind legs should always follow the front legs with a uniform bend along his body.

'Go large' Rider(s) should proceed around the outside track of the school or arena. If riding a figure, they should complete it, not repeat it, and go round the outside track.

'Gullet' The area around where the throat latch of the bridle lies, where the head attaches to the neck. The horse may show slight flexion 'in the gullet' but he must not show more bend in the head and neck than that corresponding from his body, as described above.

'In front of the leg' The term used when the horse will instantly respond to the rider's leg aid with the lightest reaction and desire to move forward.

'Jumping length' The rider shortens his stirrups by a number of holes (usually at least two and often many more) so that he can adopt a lighter seat position (or jumping position).

'Left to left' When working in an enclosed area with other riders, the code of practice is to pass any other rider you may meet left hand to left hand.

'Make much' The term used when riders are encouraged to reward their horse with a pat on the neck or a praising voice, or both, to reward him for work well done.

'Napping' The horse is showing resistance to the demands of the rider, he is not responsive to the rider and is showing a desire to 'go his own way'; often associated with the horse wanting to follow his friends back to the stable or not to leave his friends when asked to ride away on his own.

'On the aids' The term used when the horse is thoroughly obedient to the rider and able instantly to respond to the rider's messages or aids.

'Paces' The horse has four paces or 'gaits': walk, trot, canter and gallop. Training of these gaits and the development of the balance and athleticism of the horse through control and enhancement of the horse's basic paces is the discipline we call 'dressage'.

'Placing pole' A pole laid on the ground, usually in front of a jump, to assist the horse in estimating where to take off for the jump. Placing poles are less commonly used on the landing side of a jump.

'Quarter line' In a riding school 20m wide by 40m long the centre line is half way across the school (10m from outside track to centre line); the quarter line is (not surprisingly) a quarter of the way across the school, i.e. 5m in from the outside track.

'**Shorten**' The horse is asked to compress his steps and frame so that the steps cover less ground but are still energetic and springy, and the resulting picture is of a rounded, framed horse with the steps lively and slightly elevated (off the ground with a clear moment of suspension in trot and canter).

'**Three-quarter line**' In a riding school 20m wide by 40m long the centre line is half way across the school (10m from outside track to centre line); the three-quarter line is (not surprisingly) three-quarters of the way across the school, i.e. 15m in from the outside track.

'**Transition**' A change of pace. This may be from one pace to another (e.g. walk to trot, or trot to halt) or it may be a change within the pace (e.g. within the trot pace, shorter more collected steps into longer more ground-covering steps).

'**Tucked up**' Describes a horse that is slightly ill at ease with himself; may be due to onset of illness but could just be 'out of sorts'. Lower abdomen appears drawn up and tight.

'**Working in**' This refers to the activity involving the early work of the horse in a training session, where the aim is to loosen the horse, warm up his muscles, stretch him and prepare him for more serious work.

Useful Addresses

British Horse Society
Stoneleigh Deer Park
Kenilworth
Warwickshire
CV8 2XZ
tel: 08701 202244 or 01926 707700
fax: 01926 707800
website: www.bhs.org.uk
email: enquiry@bhs.org.uk

BHS Examinations Department
(address as above)
tel: 01926 707783
    01926 707784
fax: 01926 707792
email: exams@bhs.org.uk

BHS Training Department
(address as above)
tel: 01926 707820
    01926 707799
email: training@bhs.org.uk

BHS Bookshop
(address as above)
tel: 08701 201918
    01926 707762
website: www.britishhorse.com

Information for Instructors

BHS Register of Instructors

If you hold a British Horse Society teaching qualification of any level it would be wise to apply to be listed on the **BHS Register of Instructors**. Full information can be obtained from the BHS Training Office.

For an annual membership fee Registered Instructors receive insurance cover in their capacity as professional riding teachers. They also receive reduced ticket prices at all the Society's training days and conventions, including concessions for first aid and child protection training days. In addition they receive support and advice from the BHS as the national governing body for professional riding instructors in the UK.

International Trainer's Passport

Once a member of the BHS Register of Instructors, the BHSAI can also apply to hold an **International Trainer's Passport**. Issued by the BHS for British instructors but on behalf of the International Group for Equestrian Qualifications, this passport gives the holder recognition of their qualification in all the international countries which are members of the IGEQ (currently over thirty worldwide). Should you ever wish to travel and work abroad in an equestrian capacity this passport will give you valued acceptance of your ability in a foreign country. For further information regarding the International Passport, contact the Training Office at the BHS.

Further Reading

The following books and booklets can all be obtained from the BHS Bookshop.

 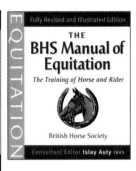 

 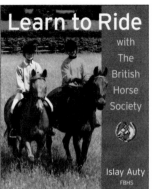  

Guide to BHS   Examinations   BHS Guide to Careers   Duty of Care
Examinations   Handbook   with Horses

College Qualifications (UK)

MSc Equine Science – A unique programme, designed to extend the depth of knowledge of equine and animal science graduates.

BSc (Hons) or BA (Hons) – This is a three-year programme; students who complete the HND or FD successfully may 'top up' for one extra year to the BSc or BA; equivalent to BHSI.

Higher National Diploma (HND) or Foundation Degree (FD) or HNC – This two-year course will develop students' technical and laboratory skills, important for handling, managing and assessing the equine athlete; equivalent to BHS Stage 4.

National Diploma – Two year, full-time course; equivalent to three 'A' levels; ideal for progressing onto HND/FD or degrees; options may include equitation, racing and stud; equivalent to BHS Stage 3.

National Certificate – One-year course; intensive programme of study; ideal for those students with some equine experience; equivalent to BHS Stage 1/2.

National Award – One-year course; covers all aspects of horse management and equitation; students could progress to second year of National Diploma; equivalent to BHS Stage 1/2.

First Diploma – Entry is for minimum age of sixteen years, two GCSEs; one-year course; basic grounding in a range of topics; progression to National Award, NC or ND; equivalent to BHS Stage 1/2.

Index

Page numbers in **bold** type refer to illustrations